Summer Reading Renaissance

Summer Reading Renaissance

An Interactive Exhibits Approach

Rita Soltan

Illustrations by Jill Reichenbach Fill

LIBRARIES
UNLIMITED

A Member of the Greenwood Publishing Group

Westport, Connecticut • London

Library of Congress Cataloging-in-Publication Data

Soltan, Rita.
    Summer reading renaissance : an interactive exhibits approach / Rita Soltan ; illustrations by
Jill Reichenbach Fill.
      p. cm.
    Includes bibliographical references and index.
    ISBN 978–1–59158–572–5 (alk. paper)
    1. Children's libraries—Activity programs—United States.   2. Children—Books and
reading—United States.   3. Reading promotion—United States.   4. Library exhibits.
5. Interactive multimedia.   I. Title.
Z718.3.S65   2008
027.62'5—dc22   2008025702

British Library Cataloguing in Publication Data is available.

Library of Congress Catalog Card Number: 2008025702
ISBN: 978–1–59158–572–5

First published in 2008

Libraries Unlimited, 88 Post Road West, Westport, CT 06881
A Member of the Greenwood Publishing Group, Inc.
www.lu.com

Printed in the United States of America

∞™

The paper used in this book complies with the
Permanent Paper Standard issued by the National
Information Standards Organization (Z39.48–1984).

10 9 8 7 6 5 4 3 2 1

The author and publisher gratefully acknowledge permission to use excerpts from the following
material:

Excerpts from Rudd, Peggy D. "Documenting the Difference: Demonstrating the Value of Libraries
Through Outcome Measurement" in *Perspectives on Outcome Based Evaluation for Libraries and
Museums*. Washington, DC: Institute of Museum and Library Services, 1999, pp. 16-22. Used with
permission.

Excerpts from Bond, Sally L., Sally E. Boyd, and Kathleen A. Rapp, Taking Stock: *A Practical Guide
to Evaluating Your Own Programs*. Chapel Hill, NC: Horizon Research, Inc. 1997.

To my family, remembering all those "veducations"
and to Joshua, my littlest summer reader—RS

To my wonderful daughters—Karlie, Lindsey,
and G. G.—JRF

Contents

Acknowledgments

I would like to recognize my former staff members who diligently worked with me to recreate and rejuvenate the summer reading program. Thank you to Jennifer Mooney Bauer, Erin Chekal, Connie Ilmer, and Laurie Scott, who willingly took the seed of an idea and, with creativity and ingenuity, allowed it to grow and blossom into a very successful interactive centers-based model. Thank you again to my friends and colleagues at the Bloomfield Township Public Library, who managed to maintain their wonderful collection through an exhaustive building renovation. And to Jill, my dedicated partner in this project, whose graphics made the development of the themes and units complete. Thank you to Barbara Ittner at Libraries Unlimited who encouraged me to write another book and to the rest of the editorial and production staff for making the book readable and, most important, useful.

Introduction

During my long career as a public children's librarian, I spent many of my summers working more like a record keeper than an inspiring reader's guide who would provide enthusiasm and enlightening suggestions to the children and families of the communities and schools within my service area. Summer's promise of relaxation and free time became overshadowed by the need to maintain skills and standards along with high circulation and program statistics. As each new summer reading theme and program loomed on my youth room's horizon, I began to question how much enjoyable and free-choice reading was really taking place within the households of the children and families I encountered each day and week. Adding increasing tally figures for books to each child's SRP registration and record card just did not convince me most kids were really participating because they were intrinsically intrigued and motivated. The faster and longer their reading logs grew, the more I suspected that books were being checked out and added without full appreciation of their content and themes. And as schools began to send in their students with "summer homework" and lists of required reading for even the lowest grade levels, I became even more concerned that the traditional library summer reading program and participation in it served more as a focal point of the school's mission than as an incentive to offer a choice in voluntary recreational summer exploration and learning. Inspired by the numerous summer vacations I spent with my own children visiting museums and locations around the Northeast and Canada, many of which had hands-on children's exhibits, I thought about how a public library could incorporate and emulate some of the general ways children are encouraged to learn and absorb new ideas through play, experimentation, and, of course, children's literature in both fictitious and informational formats.

The intent of this guidebook is to explore a new mode of library summer reading programming by implementing an innovative, family-oriented, summer-long series from an interactive exhibit/learning centers perspective. The book looks at new ways to attract summer readership and community involvement by revamping and reviving summer reading programming with a fun, creative, hands-on approach borrowed from the interactive exhibit method many museums regularly offer and from the learning centers–based focus children experience in their classrooms each day. As in the traditional SRP, one universal theme may be adopted, such as medieval times or space exploration. The program is then expanded over a 6–8 week period with a variety of exhibits or displays that invite children and their parents, guardians, or mentors to participate at their leisure during library open hours. This book provides information and explanations on:

- the rationale for recreating the summer reading program
- how libraries can learn from the museum model
- how to design an interactive centers-based program
- how to include a community volunteer team of both adults and tweens in the program
- how to measure the outcomes of a redesigned program
- themes and center units developed across a children's collection

The book is divided into two parts to incorporate background and researched information followed by detailed, fully developed exhibit and theme units. The following outline offers a description of each chapter's focus.

Part 1 Creating a Renaissance
Chapter 1 Are Library Summer Reading Programs Passé?

This chapter presents an overview of the traditional summer reading program in public libraries, their recent competition with enterprising bookstores, commercial reading incentive programs, and the new educational goals structured by federal and state mandates such as No Child Left Behind. An argument is made with logical reasons for why it is important to maintain a summer reading program in the public library and why it must be revitalized with a different approach.

Chapter 2 Energized Enthusiasm: Adapting the Museum Model and Learning Centers Approach to a Library Summer Reading Program

The philosophy behind interactive displays and learning centers is explained together with the innovative ways center participation encourages library use. The ultimate goals behind a summer reading program are restructured to rekindle and instill the desire for children and families to read together for recreation, pleasure, and their own curiosity.

Chapter 3 A Summer Reading Revival: Designing a Centers-Based Program

The basic how-tos and step-by-step approach to creating the program are detailed, including:

- an opening and closing to the season
- a simplified system of encouraging children's continued participation
- budget development
- grant money resources
- organization and continual upkeep of centers
- training of support and volunteer staff
- management in a one-librarian-staffed room
- use of today's technology to enhance the program
- cooperation with a region-wide program
- possible use of outside vendors and performers

Chapter 4 The Essential Extra: Volunteer Boosters

A very important component to this program is the organized use of tween volunteers. This keeps both ends of the youth services target audience, from preschoolers through eighth graders, busy and involved in the program. This chapter presents an explanation on how to develop a core group of "SRP Boosters" in addition to the use of adults, teens, and college students through a volunteer and school-based community service effort.

Chapter 5 Review and Reflect: Measuring Outcomes

Input and output measures have been the standard evaluation process for years. This chapter includes a discussion on how measuring outcomes has become an important added component to overall program evaluation and the application of various outcome-based evaluation models to summer reading programs.

Part 2 Sample Centers-Based Programs
Chapter 6 Interactive Intrigue

This chapter offers an introduction to three fully developed themes and exhibit/center units complete with sample projects, materials to use, suggested books for preparation, and over 75 reproducible graphics.

Chapter 7 Summer Down Under: An Awesome Aussie Experience

Fully developed program for a 6–8 week period.

Chapter 8 The Invention Convention

Fully developed program for a 6–8 week period.

Chapter 9 Traverse the Universe

Fully developed program for a 6–8 week period.

Appendix Additional Summer Reading Theme Outlines

This section provides five more suggested outlines for theme units as a base for development into full centers-based programs using the methods and techniques presented in the previous three chapters. Theme outlines follow.

ReaDiscover Ancient Egypt: The World of the Pyramids and Pharaohs
A Seafaring Summer Adventure
Let's Make Music! A Summer in Symphony and Song
Summer Safari: Animals and Folklore of the African Kingdom
Westward Ho! Catch the Pioneer Spirit

Summer reading programming continues to evolve, grow, and develop through the cooperative efforts of many. This centers-based approach combines the talents and skills of a community of librarians, volunteers, parents, teachers, and other agency leaders. It is time to rethink the library's summer reading role as one that complements the formal and informal education families and young readers include in their summer plans each year.

Part 1

Creating a Renaissance

1

Are Library Summer Reading Programs Passé?

For most people, the term *summer reading* conjures up a vision of leisure time spent in a relaxing, comfortable venue, sipping a cool drink while absorbed in a good novel, mystery, or biography. For a children's librarian, *summer reading* translates to an image of frenzied participation by scores of children and parents keeping track of reading hours and lists of books for those promised and coveted prizes. Youth librarians have been the champions of summer reading, partnering with schools, community businesses, and organizations to create programs that encourage the continuation of enjoyable and voluntary reading during the summer school-vacation period.

A Bit of History

From its inception, the public library summer reading program aimed to provide guidance with recommended reading lists while offering a variety of methods to keep children reading, recording, reporting, and returning to the library on a regular basis all summer long. Quality over quantity seemed to be the initial influence as reading lists emphasized good literature through classics and well-reviewed books. In a 1923 *Library Journal* editorial, Lydia Margaret Barrette (1923, p. 816), Librarian of the Mason City Iowa Public Library, stated: "If the child reads well enough to write a note about ten good books, as is necessary for his club work, the chances are much in his favor for developing into a reader who will have wider tastes and a deeper love of books than if no incentive were offered to try out the better books." The idea that children were the recipients of good literature through fiction was emphasized by John Cotton Dana (1920, p. 55) in his publication *A Library Primer*. His instructions on book selection for children clearly tell the practicing librarian to "buy largely for children. They are more easily trained to enjoy good books than their elders." Good books, according to Dana (p. 55), include "the wholesome novel" rather than the novel that furnishes "the silly, the weak, the sloppy, the wishy-washy, the sickly love story, the belated tract, the crude hodge-podge of stilted conversation, impossible incident, and moral platitude or moral bosh for children." Similarly, a 1929 article in *The School Review* written by

William F. Rasche (p. 204–5) summarizes what teachers and librarians of the day considered good reading:

- stories with action
- of a satisfying interest range
- with an easy to read type
- challenging for accelerated pupils
- illustrated books
- seasonal interest
- easy material for slow readers
- attractive bindings
- broadening interests in untouched fields
- excluding books that are not morally wholesome

Titles and authors that were acceptable and promoted through bookmarks and suggested lists included fairy tales and stories such as *Aesop's Fables* told anew by Joseph Jacobs (Macmillan), L. L. Brooke's *The Golden Goose Book* (Warne), and Andrew Lang's *Cinderella, or The Little Glass Slipper and Other Stories* (Longmans). Classic authors such as Louisa May Alcott, Hans Christian Andersen, and Lewis Carroll were listed side by side with nonfiction topics on history, biography, and geography (American Library Association 1922).

Vacation reading clubs, as they were referred to in the early days of library service to children, stemmed from three innovative and individual programs in three different states—the Carolyn Hewins Vacation Reading Club in Connecticut, the Carnegie Library of Pittsburgh's Summer Playground Program in Pennsylvania, and the Library League of Cleveland in Ohio (Locke 1992, p. 72–73). All three initiated activities to encourage summer reading through the availability of good books and suggested reading lists, school visit contacts prior to the last day, planned playground story hours, and library-centered book talks.

As the decades progressed, incentives to encourage the reading of good books from specific lists began to emerge, with certificates for the completion of minimal requirements to "merit badges, honor rolls and gold star lists" (Barrette 1923, p. 816). Over time, not only did the incentives and methods for achieving results change and expand, but subsequent programs such as story times, arts and crafts, themes, trivia games, contests, and special events were added. Many of these developments occurred over the years as the need to increase participation, as documented by program attendance and circulation statistics, and the competition to achieve the most books read and hours recorded overshadowed the basics of fostering a love of pleasurable and recreational reading. Concern and actual opposition to the use of competitive and incentive approaches was expressed quite early. Louise P. Latimer, Director of Work with Children at the Washington D.C. Public Library, editorialized in *Library Journal* what she called "A Regrettable Movement." She questioned the prudence of rewarding a "natural reader for what he does gladly" and remarked on the numbers of reluctant readers who have been "persuaded to love books thru [sic] required reading, and what does it profit them if they read many books and love none?" (Latimer 1923, p. 816).

With each institution's separate responsibilities and services to children, Latimer believed in the defined and separate roles of school and public library in regards to the teaching of reading versus its recreational and pleasurable aspects. Her thinking and criticism may have had some validity. In the latter quarter of the twentieth century, setting uniform goals proved to be unfair to children who struggled or lagged in their reading proficiency. New ways to encourage personal milestones with contract-based programs were tried, and the inclusion of preschool children with "Read-to-Me" versions brought in families at earlier and earlier stages. Nevertheless, based on the early models, public libraries around the country have been providing summer reading programs endorsed by teachers and parents of readers and nonreaders alike for the majority of the twentieth century and continuing into the twenty-first.

Schools and Summer Reading

Historically, the retention of reading skills and adequate scores has been a major concern and motivation for the development of required school summer reading lists and assignments. A study done over a 12-year period from 1940–1952 by Ruth Cathlyn Cook at the Laboratory School at Mankato State Teachers College in Minnesota indicated that "whenever children engaged in some systematic plan for summer reading, test results indicated significant improvement over their gain when they participated in no reading plan" (1952, p. 415). It is interesting to note that Cook's program began in 1940 with a set of required worksheets, lists of books, and words to practice. This eventually developed into a partnership program with the public library that included circus and western rodeo themes complete with certificates and the promise of a party upon completion of the program. Cook's assessment and observation that "the plans wherein children participated in group library projects and had an opportunity to share their experiences with others yielded the best scores" (p. 417) brought to light the positive outcomes of school/public library cooperation. More recently, the advent of the No Child Left Behind law and its ambitious goal of "ensuring all students are literate by 2013" has led schools and state education departments to implement their own versions of required summer reading programs with incentives that may include additional or bonus points toward autumn grades. The "homework" aspect of some of these school summer home packets has been in direct competition with the voluntary public library programs, making promotion and visibility of the library summer reading activities much more challenging for youth services staff. One way to work around this has been to gain the attention of parents through school-led parent-teacher meetings underscoring how the public library's summer activities and programs can help children meet the school's summer requirements for reading.

Summer reading loss, a definite concern for teachers, parents, and librarians, is being addressed more and more today as a major reason for overall decline in student achievement (Houck and Simon 2006). This decline is greater for children from lower socioeconomic families who tend to have less access to books and emphasis on continued literacy activities outside of school. A typical three-month summer reading gap can accumulate to a two-year loss by the time a child is in middle school (McGill-Franzen and Allington 2003, p. 18). Numerous studies have shown that voluntary reading is the single most important factor in stimulating a child's reading potential. Stephen

Krashen (2004) documents several positive aspects of a child's voluntary reading in the improvement of comprehension, vocabulary, reading speed, writing, and spelling. In compiling information and data on childhood reading interests and the significance of pleasure reading, Lynne McKechnie concludes that "opportunity to try out a book with no risks and the importance of no-cost use, the assistance of knowledgeable staff, wide choice and the ability to browse and freely choose reading material independently supports readers of all ages" (Ross, McKechnie, and Rothbauer 2006, p. 99).

The Commercial Influence

The traditional library summer reading program has also served as a model for businesses and commercial interests such as chain bookstores, coffee shops, and morning news programs. In the mid-nineties, McDonald's introduced the All-American Reading Challenge alongside Pizza Hut's Book It! Ten years later, in the summer of 2006, Jumpstart's Read for the Record was sponsored by American Eagle Outfitters, Pearson, and Starbucks. These highly commercial reading incentive programs have placed libraries more in direct competition with the businesses they had previously collaborated with in community-wide reading promotion efforts. Corporations realized that reading could be an advertising tool and a way into the desirable youth market. A study from Consumers Union, the nonprofit publisher of *Consumer Reports*, found that "reading programs are a win-win opportunity: they can earn brownie points by encouraging children to read while simultaneously marketing their products" (Reading Incentive 1995, p. 20). Other highly marketed reading incentive programs such as Accelerated Reader and its lofty prizes are incorporated into many regular school curriculums and stretched out over the summer months, while bookstores hold their own story times and reading clubs, offering coupons and promotions on a regular basis. The newest and probably best promotion to date is fast-food giant Wendy's and its summer 2007 inclusion of four Listening Library audio CDs of popular children's titles in their kids' meal bags. If getting youngsters to keep reading all year long is the genuine intent, then all efforts are welcomed. However, public libraries still have an extra responsibility to foster a love of reading by tapping into a child's natural curiosity, zoning in on keen interests, and expanding a child's view through unassigned and self-motivated reading. Children who like to read will read more, read better, and look toward new reading materials with enthusiasm.

The Impact of Incentives and Rewards

Just as Louise Latimer (1923) criticized the use of rewards to encourage "natural reading," educators today are still debating the pros and cons of providing gratification for reading in and outside of a school-based environment. Unlike schools, public libraries serve as community institutions, attracting patrons through intriguing and balanced collections, creative programs, and high-quality resources. Open and free to its residents, library usage is, nevertheless, voluntary. Despite the emphasis throughout the educational and commercial communities on children's reading development and achievement through the variety of requirements and test results or the lure of incentives and prizes, children benefit more by being encouraged to read voluntary and to think of reading as one of their recreational activities. Mandating participation can have a negative outcome if children, especially those in the lower achieving groups, are forced to read, making it seem more of a chore than a pleasure. Add to that the disappointment in not achieving a reward and reading incentives work against the purpose they are designed to accomplish. Instead, a negative message tends to be inferred by children when achieving a reward seems to be more fun than the activity of reading itself. (Caywood 1997, p. 59). In a 1999 article in *Reading Psychology*, Professors Fawson and Moore make the distinction between two kinds of motivation—extrinsic and intrinsic. "An extrinsic orientation is demonstrated when students' purpose for participation in a given activity is to receive some type of external reward. An intrinsic orientation views the participation in, and competent completion of, tasks as the desired end" (Fawson and Moore 1999, p. 326). Children who are less proficient readers and are motivated to achieve by external rewards will tend to choose the simplest or easiest way to complete a task in order to receive the reward. Literacy development may be stifled not just in terms of higher competence but in the understanding that reading may be a *chosen* activity for recreation and information. Alfie Kohn's provocative ideas in his groundbreaking book *Punished by Rewards* refers to "pop behaviorism," or the concept of "do this and you'll get that" (1993, p. 3), as a form of dehumanization by controlling the behavior of an individual. Creating an atmosphere that encourages children to read simply by the promise of a reward automatically works on the assumption that children will not read willingly for their own curiosity and enjoyment. This in itself falls back on a Skinnerian philosophy that is a form of dehumanization (Kohn 1993, p. 25–26). Forcing children to read through the promise of a reward simply undermines any intrinsic motivation for visiting the library, browsing the shelves, and actually choosing material freely without an academic purpose other than self-interest or self-stimulation.

The Need to Reinvigorate the Library Summer Reading Program

Public libraries are reinventing and recreating services continually as our world of reading and information evolves and transforms. Summer reading in the form of the traditional programming has become passé when placed next to the competition and philosophy of intrinsic versus extrinsic motivation mentioned above. But keeping kids reading over the summer is more important than ever and must be addressed anew. Working from the premise that youngsters are naturally curious and learning all the time, we need to rethink how the library can provide an enriching program environment that is nonacademic, exciting, engaging, and without rigid requirements or rules for completion. One way is to create a place where children can learn through a creative hands-on approach that invites and welcomes participation through multiple opportunities. Summer learning is usually thought of as a formal academic curriculum that is either targeted at remedial improvement or accelerated advancement. However, children can be exposed to numerous experiences outside formal school learning, particularly in the summer months, with family trips, city-run park camps, privately run day camps, typical library-oriented story hours, and grant-funded free performances. Although this kind of summer learning is more difficult for the disadvantaged family to provide, it is being addressed more closely by both schools and public libraries. Many lower-income children never visit a museum exhibit or see the inside of a public library beyond a once-a-year classroom trip. For this reason, some schools and districts are providing take-home books for the summer months with suggested ways for parents and children to read together. One such program, Super Summer Success, in Oakland County, Michigan, is an initiative to encourage the reading of six books over the summer at a child's *independent* reading level (word recognition is at least 98% and comprehension is at least 90%). Children are provided book bags with six appropriate titles for their summer reading. The project initiative provides support to both educators and parents through training, workshops, Web site help, and grant-funding resources.

Libraries are a logical place to incorporate cultural programming within a summer schedule and can easily embed alternate opportunities of learning within a summer reading program by employing a focus on interactive exhibits and learning centers. This kind of program depends on several factors that, when coordinated together, work well to bring in children with their parents or other adult family members to create, read, learn, and most of all have fun together. A well-chosen overall theme that lends itself to multi-units or subthemes is crucial to developing a series of activities that are not just craft oriented, but include puzzles, games, internet searching, hands-on experimentation, and simple projects based on a youth library's collection of materials and media resources. The interactive centers are open anytime during normal library hours and children and families are encouraged to use them at their leisure. In my past summer reading programs of this nature, parents provided very positive feedback on this approach to centers-based summer reading programming. They loved the idea of actually coming into the library to create, work on, or participate in something other than a formal record-keeping checklist. This has worked well for the child who is occupied during the day in camp or day care, as well as the child who stays home. Families come in to participate whenever time permits in their daily or weekly routine. A lotto-type recording sheet may be used (see examples in chapters 7, 8, or 9) if you wish to maintain a minimal portion of a traditional recording system. However, flexibility in satisfying the lotto sheet box directions is the key to giving kids a fair and free choice. If families are away on vacation for two weeks and have missed, for example, two weeks of activity-center content or regularly scheduled story times or book groups, substitutions of their choice are allowed. Reading time can always be swapped for any other lotto box direction. Children who are allowed to choose and read on topics they love tend to develop extensive prior knowledge that can scaffold their independent reading and help them to sustain interest (McGill-Franzen and Allington 2003, p. 58). Rotating and changing exhibits over a six-to-eight-week period with diverse components such as art, music, writing, and technology will keep young patrons interested in each new display. Finally, a strong volunteer commitment from the community, prepared with good training, will boost staff time in preparation and maintenance of interactive centers, an essential in assisting librarians and clerical staff in the implementation of a successful summer reading program.

Successful Interactive Exhibits and Learning Centers include:

- A well-chosen theme
- Accessibility during all public hours
- Flexibility to provide fair and free choice
- Regular rotation and changing of exhibits
- Diverse components such as art, music, writing, and technology
- Strong volunteer commitment with good training

If we focus more on providing a reason for children and families to come into the library, and have a renewed mission to captivate their attention in different ways than just the lure of a reward for a list of titles checked, natural interest in reading may be the overall beneficial result—and this is what teachers, parents, and librarians are continually working to attain. As cultural centers, libraries can glean much from the children's museum model that offers learning through hands-on, open-access displays on subjects particularly intriguing to children. Let us look at some of what we can do to bring this concept to the public library children's room.

References

American Library Association. 1922. *Graded Lists of Books for Children.* Chicago: American Library Association.

Barrette, Lydia Margaret. 1923. "Children's Reading Clubs." *Library Journal* (October): 816.

Caywood, Carolyn. 1997. "Eyes on the Real Prize." *School Library Journal* (April): 59.

Cook, Ruth Cathlyn. 1952. "A Dozen Summer Programs Designed to Promote Retention in Young Children." *The Elementary School Journal* 52 (March): 412–17.

Cravey, Beth Reese. "Reading for pleasure Orange Park school has summer program. (County Line)." *The Florida Times Union* (July 11, 2001): M-1. *InfoTrac Custom Newspapers.* Thomson Gale. West Bloomfield Township Public Library. June 22, 2007.

Dana, John Cotton. 1920. *A Library Primer.* Boston: Library Bureau.

Fawson, Parker C., and Sharon A. Moore. 1999. "Reading Incentive Programs: Beliefs and Practices." *Reading Psychology* 20: 325–40.

Houck, Kelly, and Anne Simon. 2003 (September), revised May 25, 2006. "Highlights of Research on Summer Reading and Effects on Student Achievement." http://www.nysl.nysed.gov/libdev/summer/research.htm.

Kohn, Alfie. 1993. *Punished by Rewards.* Boston: Houghton Mifflin.

Krashen, Stephen. 2004. *The Power of Reading.* Westport, CT: Libraries Unlimited.

Latimer. 1923. "Children's Reading Clubs; A Regrettable Movement." *Library Journal* (October): 816.

Locke, Jill. 1992. "Summer Reading Activities—Way Back When." *Journal of Youth Services in Libraries* 2 (Fall): 72–78.

McGill-Franzen, Anne, and Richard Allington. 2003. "Bridging the Summer Reading Gap." *Instructor* (May/June): 17–18, 58.

Mraz, Maryann, and Timothy V. Rasinski. "Summer Reading Loss." *The Reading Teacher* (May 2007): 784–89.

Rasche, William F. 1929. "Methods Employed to Stimulate Interests in Reading III." *The School Review* (March): 204–14.

"Reading Incentive Programs Found to Be 'Highly Commercial.'" *School Library Journal* (June 1995): 20–21.

Ross, Catherine Sheldrick, Lynne E. F. McKechnie, and Paulette M. Rothbauer. 2006. *Reading Matters: What the Research Reveals about Reading, Libraries, and Community.* Westport, CT: Libraries Unlimited.

Super Summer Success Reading Program. http://www.oakland.k12.mi.us/Departments/Early Childhood/SuperSummerSuccessReadingProgram/tabid/935/Default.aspx (accessed July 3, 2007).

2

Energized Enthusiasm: Adapting the Museum Model and Learning Centers Approach to a Library Summer Reading Program

Over the last 30 or so years, museums have developed a new approach to serving families and children using carefully designed and orchestrated interactive displays. The main objective is to encourage learning through play by tapping into a child's sense of curiosity and wonder. The Association of Children's Museums lists close to 250 children-devoted museums around the country with another 75 to open in the near future. It is a nonprofit business model that has thrived and continues to grow yearly as museums have adapted to a mission of complementing and supplementing a community's formal educational resources as provided by the schools. Some of the reasons for this high level of success and expansion have been noted by Linda R. Edeiken in her 1992 article "Children's Museums: The Serious Business of Wonder, Play, and Learning."

1. These institutions work for a broad group of people . . . first-time learners (children or adult), non-English speakers, the handicapped, etc.
2. Parents look for quality family leisure-time activities.
3. Children's museums provide a type of active, unstructured learning experience.
4. Children's museums are genuinely enjoyed by their visitors. (Edeiken 1992, p. 22)

Simultaneously, a constructivist theory of teaching through the use of learning centers as opposed to teacher-directed methods has become more commonplace in many of today's private and public classrooms. Working from the philosophies of educational psychologists like Jean Piaget and Howard Gardner, teachers employ methods that allow children to construct their own meaning through the use of prior knowledge and active participation (Piaget 1948; Gardner 1995). By examining some of the principles behind both museum interactive exhibits and classroom learning centers and gleaning some of the practical ways these approaches further informal learning, librarians can work toward invigorating a different focus for the summer reading program that will not only help to avoid the reading loss or gap educators and parents are concerned about but will energize library usage on a whole new plane.

The Museum Model in Libraries

Library-based museum-oriented exhibits are not a new phenomena. In their recent book *The Evolution of Library and Museum Partnerships*, authors Dilevko and Gottlieb make note of John Cotton Dana's use of museum-type exhibits in the Newark Free Public Library during the early 1900s as a way to "connect library and community" with the development of 74 exhibits over a 15-year period (Dilevko and Gottlieb 2004, p. 168).

In 1996, the Institute of Museum and Library Services was formed "as a federal grant-making agency dedicated to creating and sustaining a nation of learners by helping libraries and museums serve their communities" (Maher 2004, p. 3). Numerous partnership programs and exhibitions between public libraries and locally based museums have been formed under the Institute's mission to "help create vibrant, energized learning communities." At the 2003 symposium The 21st Century Learner: The Continuum Begins with Early Learning, IMLS Director Dr. Robert Sydney Martin stated the importance of "promoting developmentally appropriate, multi-sensory approaches that enhance early learning, provide training to teachers and caregivers and encourage the involvement of families throughout their children's education" (Maher 2004, p. 3).

A variety of well-designed traveling exhibits through the American Library Association's Public Programming Office have been offered for several years. One such children's initiative was the Go Figure! math exhibit, which traveled to 75 libraries around the country through February 2003 (Brandehoff 2001, p. 60). Some public libraries, like Ohio's DiscoveryWorks at the Avon Lake Public Library, offer a museum-like component to their services in a completely separate area of the building with hands-on displays that focus attention "on the objects, experience, or materials, engaging all the senses . . . enabling the visitor to discover why things happen by making them happen." These examples are collaborative efforts between libraries and museums that are designed with careful thought and attention to incorporating some of the successful ingredients of the interactive object-centered exhibit philosophy through informal learning opportunities.

Cultivating Informal Learning

Consider the word *learning*. There are in fact two kinds of learning environments that all of us have been exposed to in one way or another. There is formal learning—that of school or university education, workshop, or in-service training. There is also informal learning, which occurs continually through one's experiences based on individual interest, exposure, and participation. Children's hands-on museums address informal learning by creating environments that offer opportunities for educational interaction

through leisure and so-
cial settings. These set-
tings provide relaxed,
nonstressed atmospheres
where families and chil-
dren can choose their
activities based on self-

Interactive Displays

Include authentic content
Inspire emotional and intellectual connections
Use play, art, or experimentation

interest and motivation. Free-choice is an integral part of an informal learning environment in that it allows participants control over what they are interested in doing based
on the challenges and tasks placed at each display.

What is meant by an interactive display? For one thing, museums strive to develop content that is authentic and will inspire a child to make both an emotional
and intellectual connection. Content that helps participants make connections allows
them to develop an understanding of what is being presented. Both science- and
art-oriented museums for children today avoid the "gratuitous" type of activity that
keeps kids busy, concentrating instead on creating a responsible interactive experience. Before creating an exhibit, museum designers and educators decide specifically
what concept is to be conveyed through the activity and how it relates to the objects
presented. Creating an experience through play, art, or experimentation, with clear
directions that build from a child's prior knowledge, is the basis for this kind of participatory involvement and learning. As Maria Adams at the Institute for Learning
Innovation in Annapolis, Maryland, explains, "An interactive experience must align
directly to the outcomes that, in turn, are in direct relationship to the institutional
interactive mission statement . . . and are appropriate to the mood and tenor of the
museum" (Moreno 2003, p. 51).

Minda Borun (2002, p. 255) from The Franklin Institute Science Museum in Philadelphia introduces several multifaceted principles or characteristics that lend themselves to successful family learning in museum-based learning environments:

1. An exhibit is workable from two or three sides.
2. Several participants can use or operate the exhibit simultaneously.
3. All ages can work with the exhibit with ease.
4. The exhibit allows for sufficient stimulating content to encourage verbal
   exchanges.
5. The exhibit is suitable for different styles of learning and levels of prior
   knowledge.
6. Any written text or instruction is clearly readable and comprehensible.
7. Visitors can readily make connections between the ideas and concepts presented and their own personal insight.

Employing as many of these characteristics as possible in object-centered interactive exhibits also encourages the social aspect of visiting and exploring together through discussion, conversation, and group interaction. Deriving meaning from any interactive
exhibit is key and narrative or story provides a venue for expressing and accomplishing this. Adult reaction and participation has a greater impact on children's learning
if attention is paid to the scaffolding needs of the child, as well as how both adults

Three Overlapping Contexts and Free-Choice Learning

Personal
Socio-Cultural
Physical

(Falk and Dierking 2000, p. 13)

and children interpret the activities and directions presented (Puchner, Rapoport, and Gaskins 2001).

Informal or free-choice learning as coined by Falk and Dierking (2000, p. 13) can occur in different ways or contexts that overlap or intertwine with each other. In the personal context the learner uses prior knowledge or experience from his or her schema to make interpretations or inferences. In the socio-cultural context the learner forms an understanding and shares it within a community of learners. And in the physical context the learner develops meaning within the context of a particular object or experience outside his or her personal world. As children and families make periodic visits to museums and move from exhibit to exhibit, they are forming levels of understanding while they unconsciously work through the personal, socio-cultural, and physical contexts of each visit and experience.

An informal learning environment can also be a natural setting for specific learning and intellectual development (Paris and Hapgood, 2002). The simple act of viewing and interacting with a variety of objects promotes a visual literacy when children are allowed to handle, assemble, or experiment in a hands-on, directed way. Intrinsic motivation is encouraged when topics focus on the interests and curiosities of the intended audience. Children develop an aesthetic appreciation for what is presented to them in a way that is different from the efferent kind of learning that comes with curriculum-based formal instruction. Through family and group participation, children learn collaborative skills. And most importantly, the way children synthesize and verbalize their different exhibit experiences helps them explore their own world, interests, and identities (Paris and Hapgood 2002, p. 51). The "reading of objects" as defined by van Kraayenoord and Paris (2002) incorporates and strengthens the same skills of reading text. As with the reading of text, a reader "must decode objects, make sense of objects, read the stories of objects, engage in the shared reading of objects and be involved in reflective, never-ending stories" (van Kraayenoord and Paris 2002, p. 232).

Finally, in our modern technological environment, C. Olivia Frost at the University of Michigan addresses the benefits of learning from objects that are presented in digital format either through online museum sites or on-site museum digital displays. While digital displays provide a replication of the original, they nevertheless expand the possibility of providing information to a wider audience with "contextual information that can enrich the viewing experience" (Frost 2002, p. 93). At the same time, they must be used in conjunction with original artifacts and with the guidance of an educator to "stimulate interest in a broad array of viewers and result in greater levels of engagement with the real objects in museums" (Frost 2002, p. 93).

Schools, Learning Centers, and the Principles of the Museum Model

The constructivist theory of creating meaning through active participation is the basis for much of the philosophy behind a centers-based classroom environment.

Learning centers offer diverse learners ways to practice, implement, or discover skills and knowledge in addition to the sole teacher-directed focus of a traditional classroom

Elements of a Centers-Based Classroom

Hands-on activities with small groups or mini-lessons
Differentiated learning with auditory, visual, kinesthetic, multisensory tasks
Meaningful play to learn

setting. They provide additional instruction by making the learning of concepts more exciting through hands-on activities and experiments coupled with small group or individualized mini-lessons to achieve genuine understanding. In a centers-based classroom, teachers "act as true facilitators of learning rather than transmitters of facts and formulas" and help "children develop habits of learning that last a lifetime" (Sloane 1998–1999). These classrooms are more exciting learning environments through differentiated education with auditory, visual, kinesthetic, and multisensory tasks. The reality that children learn at different paces, have different interests and needs, and become more motivated when they are given the chance to make choices based on their interests adds further support to the rationale for centers-based learning. And while a classroom exhibits formal learning, providing choices encourages a sense of trust and respect and fosters a more meaningful relationship between student peers and teaching staff.

Play to learn is another important element of a centers-based approach. "Play is the natural vehicle by which children learn" (Bottini and Grossman 2005, p. 276). Young children play and learn simultaneously when concepts and ideas are presented through simulated situations in which they can explore and experiment. When children construct their own knowledge through a firsthand approach, they are better able to retain it and then transfer it to another context. Providing "multiple opportunities to engage in rich, culturally sensitive and meaningful play" encourages children to develop competencies in areas of creativity, literacy skills, social settings, and an overall trust in their personal capabilities (Kieff and Casbergue 2000, p. 9–10).

When we compare the two environments—formal classroom centers-based learning and informal children's museum interactive exhibit learning—similar positive outcomes can be noted for each as a participatory learning approach.

- Children learn through direct experience.
- Children are provided choices in which to work from their prior interests and knowledge.
- Real understanding occurs in a context filled with authentic possibilities.
- Community learning is encouraged through social interaction among peers and families.
- Creative thinking skills are developed through problem-solving techniques with visual, auditory, and multisensory opportunities.

Summer Reading Programs and the Interactive Display and Centers Model

If we consider preventing summer reading loss as one of the major missions of library-run summer reading programs, together with the overall objective of instilling a life-long love of reading, then developing programs that inspire reading through an interactive centers-based approach is a way to subversively, if you will, attract children to topics and reading material by appealing to their natural curiosity, sense of wonder, and play. Libraries are natural places to create informal learning environments that work within the three overlapping contexts of learning—the personal, the socio-cultural, and the physical. Just as museum educators and classroom teachers determine specific goals for each exhibit theme or curriculum unit when creating interactive displays and centers, librarians must also evaluate and decide on specific outcomes they hope to achieve with a new interactive centers-based format for a summer reading program. These outcomes can be addressed within each context of learning as follows:

The Personal Context—To evoke the emotional response of doing something different and intriguing to make the library visit and participation in a summer reading program an affective experience.

- A choice of interactive activities that change over the summer period allows personal control over how children wish to participate.
- Well-planned displays with clear directions will encourage successful endeavors and spark enthusiasm and personal pleasure.
- Free-choice participation leads to free-choice reading on a related topic of personal interest based on a child's prior knowledge and experience.
- Content-rich, intriguing, creative, and unique concepts will encourage a child's natural sense of curiosity and quest for understanding.

The Socio-Cultural Context—To create a convivial and communal experience by encouraging group participation at the centers with friends and family.

- Libraries are social places and can offer a venue to learn by interacting with others.
- Fun/play is stimulated at the centers through cooperative efforts with peers and family members.
- Reading, conversation, discussion, and experimentation with peers and family extend the purpose of the library summer visit beyond listing the number of books and hours read.

The Physical Context—To place the focus of summer reading programming throughout the youth room by combining centers with the library's collection of materials, objects, and books.

- Participation encourages a productive outcome of learning through art, music, puzzles, games, and, of course, reading in both real and digital or virtual formats.
- Center participation can be extended to the home with continued suggested ideas for reading, investigating, playing, and creating.

Like museums, this kind of library informal learning can both supplement and complement the formal learning in the community's schools. The interactive centers-based summer reading program can retain, build, and strengthen reading interests, thereby maintaining the thinking and cognitive skills children have developed throughout the year. More importantly, like museums, libraries will develop into another resource of engaged, participatory education for children and families within the community's list of established institutions. The key to success, however, is in the design and implementation of these themed summer reading exhibits and centers.

References

Borun, Minda. 2002. "Object-Based Learning and Family Groups." In *Perspectives on Object-Centered Learning in Museums*, ed. Scott G. Paris, p. 245–60. Mahwah, NJ: Lawrence Erlbaum Associates.

Bottini, Michael, and Sue Grossman. 2005. "Center-Based Teaching and Children's Learning: The Effects of Learning Centers on Young Children's Growth and Development." *Childhood Education* (Annual Theme): 274–77.

Brandehoff, Susan. 2001. "Go Figure! Exhibit Brings Kids and Calculations Together." *American Libraries* (December): 60–61.

Dilevko, Juris, and Lisa Gottlieb. 2004. *The Evolution of Library and Museum Partnerships: Historical Antecedents, Contemporary Manifestations, and Future Directions.* Westport, CT: Libraries Unlimited.

Edeiken, Linda R. 1992. "Children's Museums: The Serious Business of Wonder, Play, and Learning." *Curator* 35 (1): 21–27.

Falk, John H., and Lynn D. Dierking. 2000. *Learning from Museums: Visitor Experiences and the Making of Meaning.* Walnut Creek, CA: Altimira Press.

Frost, Olivia C. 2002. "When the Object is Digital: Properties of Digital Surrogate Objects and Implications for Learning." In *Perspectives on Object-Centered Learning in Museums*, ed. Scott G. Paris, p. 79–94. Mahwah, NJ: Lawrence Erlbaum Associates.

Gardner, Howard. 1995. *The Unschooled Mind.* New York: Basic Books.

Kieff, Judith E., and Renee M. Casbergue. 2000. *Playful Learning and Teaching: Integrating Play into Preschool and Primary Programs.* Boston: Allyn and Bacon.

Maher, Mary, ed. 2004. *The 21st Century Learner: The Continuum Begins with Early Learning, Symposium Report.* Washington, DC: Association of Children's Museums.

Moreno, Cynthia, Molly Polk, and Lisa Buck. 2003. "The Dilemma of Interactive Art Museum Spaces." *Art Education* 56 (5): 42–52.

Paris, Scott. G., and Susanna E. Hapgood. 2002. "Children Learning with Objects in Informal Learning Environments." In *Perspectives on Object-Centered Learning in Museums*, ed. Scott G. Paris, p. 37–54. Mahwah, NJ: Lawrence Erlbaum Associates.

Piaget, Jean. 1948. *To Understand is to Invent.* New York: Viking.

Puchner, Laurel, Robyn Rapoport, and Suzanne Gaskins. 2001. "Learning in Children's Museums: Is It Really Happening? *Curator* 44 (3): 237–59.

Sloane, Marie W. 1998–1999. "Learning Resource Centers: Engaging Primary Students." *Childhood Education* 75 (2): 76–82.

Speaker, Kathryne McGrath. 2001. "Interactive Exhibit Theory: Hints for Implementing Learner-Centered Activities in Elementary Classrooms." *Education* 121 (3): p. 610–14.

van Kraayenoord, Christina E., and Scott G. Paris. 2002. "Reading Objects." In *Perspectives on Object-Centered Learning in Museums*, ed. Scott G. Paris, p. 215–34. Mahwah, NJ: Lawrence Erlbaum Associates.

Web Sites

The Association of Children's Museums. http://www.childrensmuseums.org/visit/us_members.htm (accessed July 19, 2007).

Avon Lake Public Library: Discovery Works. http://www.alpl.org/DiscoveryWorks/Default.asp# (accessed June 19, 2008).

Institute of Museum and Library Services. http://www.imls.gov/about/about.shtm (accessed June 19, 2008).

3

A Summer Reading Revival: Designing a Centers-Based Program

It's mid-August and your summer finale has just ended. The thought of another summer program is one you would like to shelve, at least until all the autumn leaves have been raked and bundled. Planning ahead for summer reading often begins early into the new school year. Planning ahead for a centers-based summer reading program requires working out a more detailed summer-long concept. It entails a schedule of exhibits smoothly transitioning from one week to the next with your coordinated direction between staff and volunteers.

A Workable Plan

Restructuring a summer reading program begins with an evaluation of how your community has participated in the past; what resources in terms of space, materials, funding, staff, and volunteers are available; and what specific contexts you would like to create that will provide authentic opportunities for informal or free-choice learning.

Noting the Past

Take a look at your library's summer reading history for the last five years. A compilation of circulation and participation/program attendance statistics can help you determine not just which collections are favored during the summer months but average ages of former participants and which programs attracted a higher attendance. Another point to note is whether your schools have included required summer reading assignments and how your library has serviced this need. Were you able to participate with community organizations and businesses or did they offer competing reading incentive programs? An evaluation of this sort can help you work toward a centers-based approach that can emphasize aspects of your collection in intriguing ways and draw in a population that has previously been reticent. Your evaluation should also take into account positive aspects of your past programs that you may want to keep and incorporate into your revived summer reading plan. You may want to continue to hold an opening day introductory program and a finale party, especially if they have been successful in instilling initial enthusiasm and community camaraderie. The opening day can be a wonderful way to introduce your new centers and exhibits concept simultaneously or following your grand opening session. You may want to create two centers or interactive exhibits with simple activities for families to try as part of the day's plan.

Analyzing previous benchmark methods for participating summer readers can help you determine how to include a simplified system or whether you even want to have anything as formal as in previous years. Remember, benchmarks can lead to incentives, which can keep your program from moving away from a competitive focus. However, you may still choose to maintain a limited incentive version by using a game-sheet approach with small incremental steps to keep kids coming back for such things as lottery prize drawings and Friends of the Library bookstore coupons. Sample game sheets and suggested rules are included in the themed programs in chapters 7–9.

A word on rewarding parents and/or caregivers—they are the keys to a successful interactive centers-based program since a majority of the exhibits you create work well when used by families together. Encouraging parents and caregivers to participate with their children is extremely important in a program that requires self-directed engagement. Acknowledging them for their hard work in maintaining interest and a connection to the program emphasizes and rewards parents and caregivers for the role they must play in their child's summer reading progression. Lottery entries with each daily or weekly visit can provide weekly chances at lotto drawings. Opportunities to enter separate pools for parents and kids, with a chance for parents to win a limited number of donated prizes of dinner for two at a local restaurant or movie vouchers, keeps everyone interested in returning each week. Chances to win can increase the more times a family returns and enters their name in the drawing. For example, one to two family names can be pulled from the lotto boxes each Friday before closing and announced the following morning on the library's Web site and with a phone call to the lucky winners.

One of the best and widely used noncompetitive incentives is a Friends of the Library–sponsored paperback summer reading "bookstore cart" allowing children to "buy" or choose a book they may add to their home library when they have achieved a particular milestone in the program. You may also wish to acknowledge gains with a completion certificate at the end of the summer. Regardless of the motivational system you employ, it is the lure of the centers you create that will hopefully become the stimulus behind participation rather than the benchmarks and incentives you offer.

Creating a Scheduled Outline

Once your evaluation of previous years' programs is complete, outlining a schedule for the six-to-eight-week forthcoming summer period becomes easier to organize into weekly or biweekly units and corresponding exhibits or interactive centers. Themes can be worked into three or four units and subthemes that are then developed with two to four exhibits per unit. I have included typical programming such as story hours within each week's or unit's schedule, as these can be ongoing and incorporate staff time and center supervision accordingly. A generic schedule below is an example of a full summer-long program. This schedule reflects four units over an eight-week period with one to four interactive centers for each unit that can be rotated or displayed simultaneously depending on the amount of exhibit space available. Units can include less than four exhibits depending on budget, staff preparation, maintenance time, and space limitations. (See chapter 6 for designing a specific theme-based sample schedule and program.)

Centers-Based Summer Reading Program Schedule Outline

1. Grand opening program to include
   a. Registration (may include a give-away packet with game sheet and possible small theme-related item)
   b. Introduction to overall theme
   c. Possible outside performer
   d. Two interactive centers (these can be more generic to your summer theme and available in your program/community room area for the open house only)

2. Weeks One and Two
   a. Unit 1
      i. Interactive Centers 1–4
   b. Regular Story Hour programming
   c. Possible Special or Performance programming
   d. Book Discussion programming

3. Weeks Three and Four
   a. Unit 2
      i. Interactive Centers 1–4
   b. Regular Story Hour programming
   c. Possible Special or Performance programming
   d. Book Discussion programming

4. Weeks Five and Six
   a. Unit 3
      i. Interactive Centers 1–4
   b. Regular Story Hour programming
   c. Possible Special or Performance programming
   d. Book Discussion programming

5. Weeks Seven and Eight
   a. Unit 4
      i. Interactive Centers 1–4
   b. Regular Story Hour programming
   c. Possible Special or Performance programming
   d. Book Discussion programming

6. Finale Program
   a. Performance
   b. Grand lottery drawings for parent and child participants
   c. Presentation of Certificates

The Floor Plan

Before deciding the number of centers you wish to include for each week's unit, take stock of your youth room's physical layout and create a floor plan. This helps in the overall management of your exhibits and interactive display area. Keeping the exhibits area within the context of your youth library is a good idea for several reasons. It keeps the center of attention within the youth library's area, thereby facilitating staff monitoring and promotion. Children can freely choose their level of participation when they come in to select books or take part in other regularly scheduled programming. Often, the excitement of one family's involvement may attract others to the center area to watch and then join in. Several reading tables can be placed together, or if you have more space, you may decide to stagger one or two exhibits at various separate stations. Do not forget to make use of computer stations as designated Internet or software-based centers for your digital and virtual corresponding exhibits.

Design Matters

Developing and designing centers that are exciting and that can facilitate informal learning requires foresight and careful consideration of the specific content and concepts you wish to convey along with age appropriateness, feasibility of presentation, and how participants will react and respond. Taking cues from the museum model explored earlier, you can apply certain aspects to each exhibit's plan and execution.

- Create responsible centers and displays that are appropriate to the goals you have developed for your summer reading program and theme.
- Make the experience fun and enjoyable.
- Allow participants to make connections from their personal knowledge and interests.
- Offer choices that will be accessible to different learners, learning styles, and ages.
- Layer difficult concepts so that different participants may work at different levels.
- Create readable, easy-to-understand directions and information.
- Make the center multifamily and multiuser friendly.

If you are developing a unit with two to four centers, make sure at least one is directed at younger users while the others are doable from all ages with or without adult help. You may also do this within the context of one center by offering choices or a variety of activities designed for older and younger abilities respectively. For example, in a center focusing on industrial technology and the significance of the railroad (see chapter 8, Invention Convention—Weeks 3 & 4, Gallery of Trains), children are provided with books for older and younger reading and listening levels and are offered separate art-based projects to extend the history of trains. Older children may create a series of drawings on the different kinds of train technology from an Ed Emberley drawing book while younger may create a simple train collage from a basic geometric template. Stay cognizant of children with special needs. In this case, try to include something that is easily accessible with minimal help from an adult or that requires interaction

Library Floor Plans

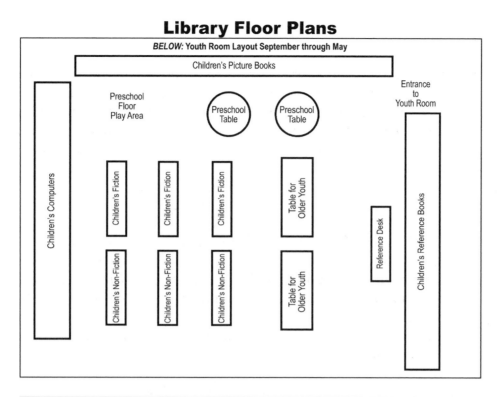

BELOW: Youth Room Layout September through May

Children's Picture Books

Preschool Floor Play Area

Preschool Table

Preschool Table

Entrance to Youth Room

Children's Computers

Children's Fiction

Children's Fiction

Children's Fiction

Table for Older Youth

Children's Non-Fiction

Children's Non-Fiction

Children's Non-Fiction

Table for Older Youth

Reference Desk

Children's Reference Books

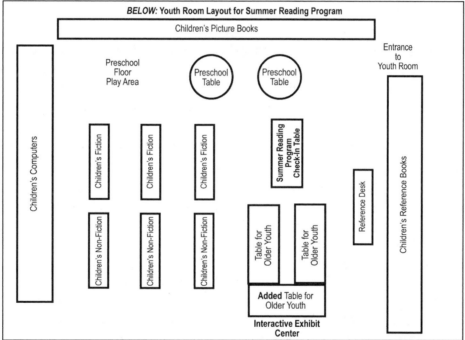

BELOW: Youth Room Layout for Summer Reading Program

Children's Picture Books

Preschool Floor Play Area

Preschool Table

Preschool Table

Entrance to Youth Room

Children's Computers

Children's Fiction

Children's Fiction

Children's Fiction

Summer Reading Program Check-In Table

Children's Non-Fiction

Children's Non-Fiction

Children's Non-Fiction

Table for Older Youth

Table for Older Youth

Added Table for Older Youth

Interactive Exhibit Center

Reference Desk

Children's Reference Books

between an adult and child. An all-inclusive goal of the interactive center allows children with special needs opportunities to work with the exhibits at their own pace and level of comprehension. Employing the seven characteristics as noted by Minda Borun (2002, p. 255) in the previous chapter is a wonderful way to test the feasibility and learning potential of all your exhibits and centers. Do your centers have some of these features?

- Can a family or group work the exhibit from two or three sides?
- Can several participants use or operate the exhibit simultaneously?
- Can both children and adults use the materials comfortably?
- Are directions readable and easily understood in short simple sections?
- Does the center stimulate a level of ideas for verbal exchanges and discussion?
- Does the center or concept presented appeal to different learning styles and levels of prior knowledge?
- Can the concepts and ideas help participants make connections to their lives and the world around them?

Financing and Budgeting

The next important consideration is budget and funding for your overall program. Developing centers requires the available use of some basic supplies or staples to extend the concepts and ideas presented through the units. Working out your designs ahead helps to anticipate the type and quantity of supplies you will need to stock each unit for each week. Working from your collection of books and media, choose some basic arts and crafts materials to add to whatever objects, projects, and experiments you develop for your themes and units. And since centers are open during open library hours, fold in some extra dollars for these basic supplies. However, it need not be an unlimited offer of paper, glue, and crayons. Limits can be set gently by allowing children to use a maximum number of centers in one day and to do the project or experiment only once for each center they work at. If you participate with a library cooperative, supplies can also be ordered more cheaply in bulk or you might want to look into the possibility of an arts and crafts scrap vendor or discount warehouse in your area. Also remember to include funding for volunteer training and recruitment.

Increasing Your Funds

There are a number of ways to add to your tax-based allocation and increase your pool of funds. Search out local grants through existing community relationships and cultivate new ones with agencies interested in children's and family literacy. An initial source to explore is the Friends of the Library. FOLs have been instrumental in helping to enhance quality and quantity of services in public libraries. Like a school's Parent Teacher Organization, the FOL group can be one of the largest supporters of your newly revised summer reading program. Establish an ongoing relationship with your FOL board members and attend their meetings as often as you can. It is important to let them in on your ideas and objectives on a regular basis. You can do this by asking to speak for 5 or 10 minutes every season to keep them abreast of services. This way,

Following is a sample budget outline for a six-to-eight-week summer reading centers-based program.

Room Decorations _____

Opening Day

    Refreshments_____
    Performer _____
    Give away bags/items _____

12–16 Centers/Basic Supplies _____

    Staples should include glue, paper, kraft paper rolls, paper plates, crayons, markers, child safe scissors, etc.
    Other _____
    (commercially prepared games, puzzles, etc.)

2 Mid-summer special programs/performers _____

Closing Day

    Refreshments_____
    Performer _____

Printing of game sheets, rules, certificates _____

Lotto prizes _____

    Donations for parent dinners, movie tickets, etc.

Bookstore Cart

    Paperback books _____

Volunteer/Booster Training Session _____

    Booster marketing/printing _____

when you work out a proposal for your new summer reading program, your previous relationship will be an asset and the FOL will be more receptive to your funding needs.

As with any grant request, an introductory proposal is the best way to begin the fund-seeking conversation with your FOL. Your proposal should begin with the reasons or need to change your existing summer reading program to one that is centers based. Include a rationale for the three legs of education in a community.

The schools provide formal education while museums and libraries each supplement and complement the school's curriculum through informal education. Summer reading programs fall under the library's informal education leg, particularly to help prevent summer reading loss. To boost your argument and rationale you may want to cite some statistics from the American Library Association's recent National Survey Results done by KRC Research. An online summary is available (http://www.ala.org/ala/ors/reports/KRC_Detailed_Slides.pdf) and incorporates some very positive results for public library usage, image, value, and benefits, and in particular, parental expectations for services to children. For example, 68 percent of parents surveyed indicated that they visit the public library to check out materials while 41 percent came because "The Library gives us something to do together" (ALA, p. 19). When broken down by age demographics, 71 percent of parents of young children visit to check out materials while 46 percent enjoy doing something together (ALA, p. 20). Similarly, 94 percent valued libraries as places for lifetime learning (ALA, p. 32), with 82 percent

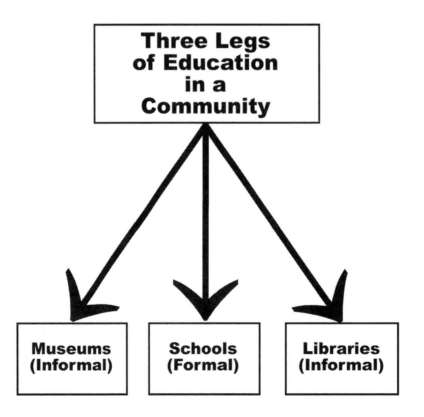

indicating cultural programs and activities as a major benefit (ALA, p. 33). Most importantly, 90 percent felt the library played an important role in the community and to the family's education (ALA, p. 35). Finally, an overwhelming 95 percent felt that libraries were very important as institutions that "contribute to public education, provide life-long learning opportunities, and free resources" (ALA 2006, p. 42).

Use previous SRP statistics and outcomes to state your goals and objectives clearly and succinctly on how you are targeting new participants to join traditional users, how family literacy is one of your intended goals, and how your exhibits/interactive centers will be designed, staffed, and maintained through collaborative staff and volunteer efforts. When presenting an overall budget in your proposal, remember to target one or two things you wish the FOL to help you fund that are important for the overall implementation of your revived program. This can be extra dollars for center supplies or paperback books for the SRP bookstore cart or the opening or closing day programs. Be sure to include a plan for evaluating the success of your new program and how you plan to report back to your FOL. Traditionally, FOLs have been very receptive to helping children participate and extend their library experience. From participation in the national Books for Babies campaign to volunteering in a variety of literacy-targeted programs centered at the library, the Friends of the Library can be the best and most supportive advocate for your newly designed summer initiative.

Another avenue to probe in the community is the variety of local civic groups and foundations interested in working closely as a partner with your library. Is there a local Lions Club or Kiwanis group? Does the local Rotary Club provide small grants for literacy-based projects? There are thousands of community foundations all across the country, diverse in terms of size and scope of interests. A little research through a foundations directory most probably housed in the reference room may highlight one or two smaller grant possibilities for your program. An even easier way to research community foundation possibilities is through the Grantsmanship Center Web site (http://tgci.com/index.shtml), which will lead you to a large U.S. map from which you may find local foundations in your state and community. Publishers are another resource to tap for innovative program development, such as the ALSC/BWI Reading Program Grant (http://www.ala.org/ala/alsc/awardsscholarships/profawards/bookwholesalers/bookwholesalers.htm). Pooling your funding from a couple of resources such as your FOL and a community organization or foundation will help to develop your centers and overall program with a substantial amount of supplies, materials, and activities. Other resources for grants and writing grant proposals are listed at the end of this chapter.

A Group Effort

Once you have drafted ideas for your summer reading theme's four units, designing and implementing each of the 12–16 centers need not

Additional Funding Resources

Friends of the Library
Local civic groups
Local foundations
Corporate interests
Publisher grants

Enlist Administrative Support

Keep supervisors informed of ideas and plans
Develop a concise proposal
Use bullet points for goals and objectives
Assure other regular work will continue

be overwhelming if you enlist extra help from fellow youth librarians, support staff, library pages, and volunteers. An average mid-sized library serving a population of 50,000 employs 24 FTE, with one third holding MLS degrees.[1] It can be assumed that of these eight FTE librarians, at least two are assigned to youth and YA services. Combining talent, initiative, and skill together with extra able hands makes it easy to divide the workload of designing, creating, and rotating your centers. Convincing everyone that your museum concept for a revived summer reading program is a joint effort goes more smoothly, of course, if you maintain a good relationship with everyone on the staff, from director down to maintenance crew. Keep your supervisor informed of how you plan to revive and change your next summer reading program. As with your FOL group, develop a concise proposal with well-thought-out bullet points and a list of goals and objectives. In addition, if you plan to encourage help from other departments, assure supervisors that other work will not be neglected with several people pitching in. You may want to introduce your program at a general staff meeting or entice some of your more creative clerical or support staff to take a role in the plans. If your FTE youth staff is made up of a majority of part-timers, this can be more advantageous in that the workload can be divided between more people. For example, a youth department with one full-time department head and two part-time 20-hour-per-week librarians can develop an eight-week program with each librarian taking responsibility for four centers over the course of a four-unit summer to include 12 centers.

Help from your pages, clerical staff volunteers, and community volunteers adds the extra assistance to create and implement your professional interactive exhibits.

Libraries serving smaller populations with smaller numbers of youth professional FTEs can choose to tailor the program with fewer units or centers depending on staff time and space allotment for their youth area. Even a very limited centers-based program for a one-librarian-staffed youth area can be accomplished with fewer units

Librarians' Schedule

	Wk 1 & 2	Wk 3 & 4	Wk 5 & 6	Wk 7 & 8
	Unit 1	*Unit 2*	*Unit 3*	*Unit 4*
Librarian 1	Center 1	Center 1	Center 1	Center 1
Librarian 2	Center 2	Center 2	Center 2	Center 2
Librarian 3	Center 3	Center 3	Center 3	Center 3

over a shorter time frame that exchanges two centers perhaps every other week. Whatever the number of centers you choose to create and maintain, exchanging them at least biweekly keeps patrons interested in returning for continued participation.

Another way to increase your ability to create interactive centers with little staff and time available is to work together with counterpart youth staff within your cooperative. Many one-librarian-staffed situations can benefit from this sort of co-op sharing. With 76 percent of public libraries sharing membership in a federation or cooperative service, it can be quite practical to form committees within a cooperative to research, design, and put in place easily reproducible centers that can be dispensed across the region.[2]

With your group of center designers and workers in tow, you are now ready to divide the workload and provide some basic training and discussion. Encourage staff to do some research on their topic in order to develop and organize their particular centers. Hand out a summarized sheet of the design matters mentioned above so everyone is on board with your new program concept. Create a prototype of each center and test it out with each other to see if it is feasible or has unexpected problems. And most important, encourage staff to keep it as simple, inexpensive, and easily supplied with basic materials as possible.

Promoting Your Summer Reading Renaissance

During the month of May, most children's and youth services librarians are on a traveling road show throughout the community's schools promoting the upcoming summer reading program and club. This can range from classroom storytelling to large-group-assembly skits librarians perform to entice and encourage participation as the school year comes to a close. A supportive district and faculty will most certainly welcome this promotion, but more often than not the children will enjoy the guest visitors for the moment and, days later, lose the connection librarians work so hard to create. Similarly, brochures and flyers passed out during class time have a minimal chance of making it home to mom and dad for renewed emphasis. This direct-marketing type of campaign is traditional and has some positive effect, but more and more, librarians need to develop a renewed focus and strategy when it comes to promoting a completely different concept for their summer reading renaissance.

In the 1980s the library community began to reinvent itself in terms of promotion by applying the bookstore model. New display shelving, popular subject headings, and multiple copies with covers facing prospective readers changed the physical look and accessibility of collections for many community public libraries. The idea that popular reading could be as accessible and available to patrons as any bookstore changed the public's perception of borrowing versus buying when they did not have to wait in long reserve lines for the one or two copies of a hot title. Merchandizing library collections brought in readers, both young and old, confident that their coveted titles of the moment would be waiting for them on the shelves. The bookstore model stuck for many libraries, changing the perception of public libraries throughout the last two decades of the twentieth century. As Malcolm Gladwell explains in his book *The Tipping Point,* "the tipping point is the biography of an idea, and the idea is very simple" (2000, p. 7).

It was a "tipping point" in library service that resulted in higher usage and circulation statistics and better financial support. Much of this change in service developed throughout the professional community through word-of-mouth that filtered down to the public as library professionals reinvented their approach to shelving and displaying their collections. The idea of merchandized collections had what Gladwell calls "stickiness" because it caught on and encouraged librarians across the country to recreate the way collections were housed and offered.

Reviving a traditional summer reading program to an interactive centers-based and museum-model approach has that stickiness potential—it can be an experience that is memorable and is repeated often. It is a concept that can be newly innovative and bolster children, parents, teachers, and librarians to think of the library in general and summer reading clubs in particular as an extension of a community's educational and cultural contribution. In concert with a marketing campaign for your revived program through the traditional avenue of school visits and newsletter/brochure/flyer announcements, you need to create "buzz" about your fresh, new idea for summer reading. You need to get the interested stakeholders in your community—kids, parents, grandparents, teachers, community leaders, and such—to start talking about your novel concept and thereby spread the word.

Buzzmarketing is not a serendipitous happening but rather a carefully maneuvered strategy commonplace in today's world of advertising. It is about getting "people to talk about your stuff," as Mark Hughes states in his book *Buzzmarketing* (2005). Begin the word-of mouth promotion from community leader to teacher to parent to child by telling a well-crafted story *you develop* focused on how and why your new SRP will add to the community's list of positive summer pastimes. Repeating your story to a media contact further boosts your promotion objective, but as Dave Balter and John Butman point out in their book *Grapevine* (2005), credibility is the key to a word-of-mouth campaign and most powerful when delivered by ordinary people. A good example of how word of mouth can propel a new program forward is the mother/daughter book clubs that developed a few years ago from an idea in a particular home and community. Pairing middle-school girls with their moms in a book-discussion program began to take hold in public libraries and schools when the idea was reported through the media, a published book, and finally word-of-mouth endorsement throughout the parental community. This is the sort of buzz you want to create in the spring, which will continue through the summer months as families begin to work their way through the variety of exhibits and centers.

Old-fashioned word-of-mouth publicity can also spread rapidly through online communities. Web 2.0 communities such as blogs, wikis, listservs, and discussion groups are popping up every day and are the fastest way to spread news and opinions through an online social network. If your library's Web site has included a

Buzzmarketing

Tell your well-crafted story early and often to: stakeholders, media, Web 2.0 community
Keep your story credible
Update your story often
Repeat it to all periodically

youth services blog, this is the place to start. Latch on to other web communities within your parent-teacher organizations, church groups, state and local educational associations, library cooperatives in your region, and other online venues to begin to spread your story. Keep a running weekly update on the SRP's planning progress on the library's blog and Web site throughout the spring to generate initial interest and, as the summer approaches, send updates to your local online groups.

The virtual and face-to-face grapevine throughout your community will help build a clean, refreshed perception of a library summer reading program. Begin to tell your story early and repeat its message with every contact you make, both at the reference desk and outside the library building. Your buzzmarketing will also achieve another purpose. It will help you generate interest in recruiting a volunteer crew to help implement and run your centers-based summer reading renaissance.

Notes

1. Source: U.S. Department of Education, National Center for Education Statistics, Federal-State Cooperative System (FSCS) for Public Library Data, Public Libraries Survey (PLS), FY 2004. http://nces.ed.gov/pubs2006/2006349.pdf.

2. Source: U.S. Department of Education, National Center for Education Statistics, Federal-State Cooperative System (FSCS) for Public Library Data, Public Libraries Survey (PLS), FY 2004. http://nces.ed.gov/pubs2006/2006349.pdf.

Grants Resources

Bayley, Linda. "Grant Me this: How to Write a Winning Grant Proposal." *School Library Journal* (September 1995): p. 126–28.

The Foundation Directory. New York, Foundation Center; distributed by Columbia University Press, 2006.

Grantsmanship Center. http://tgci.com/index.shtml.

Hall-Ellis, Sylvia D., et al. *Grantsmanship for Small Libraries and School Library Media Centers.* Westport, CT: Libraries Unlimited, 1999.

Hall-Ellis, Sylvia D. and Ann Jerabek. *Grants for School Libraries.* Westport, CT: Libraries Unlimited, 2003.

References

Balter, Dave, and John Butman. 2005. *Grapevine: The New Art of Word-of-Mouth Marketing.* New York: Portfolio/Penguin Group.

Borun, Minda. 2002. "Object-Based Learning and Family Groups." In *Perspectives on Object-Centered Learning in Museums,* ed. Scott G. Paris, p. 245–60. Mahwah, NJ: Lawrence Erlbaum Associates.

Gladwell, Malcolm. 2000. *The Tipping Point: How Little Things Can Make a Big Difference.* New York: Little Brown.

Hughes, Mark. 2005. *Buzzmarketing: Get People to Talk about Your Stuff.* New York: Portfolio/Penguin Group.

Karsh, Ellen, and Arlen Sue Fox. 2006. *The Only Grant-Writing Book You'll Ever Need.* Second Edition. New York: Carroll & Graf Publishers.

Web Sites

ALSC/BWI Reading Program Grant. http://www.ala.org/ala/alsc/awardsscholarships/ profawards/bookwholesalers/bookwholesalers.htm.

American Library Association. KRC Research @ your library American Library Association: National Survey Results. February 2006, http://www.ala.org/ala/ors/reports/krcde tailedslides.pdf.

Grantsmanship Center. http://tgci.com/index.shtml.

4

The Essential Extra: Volunteer Boosters

Volunteerism plays a significant role in the function and services of our public and school libraries. Historically, many smaller city and town libraries began through the organization of volunteer literary leagues and clubs. The groundwork for the establishment of many of the major library systems in the United States can be traced to voluntary efforts coupled with large endowments from major donors such as Andrew Carnegie and the Astor Foundation. Many of our present-day libraries are overseen and operate under the support of voluntary boards. "Board activity can be seen as one of the oldest forms of volunteer service [in libraries]" (Wyly 1992). Volunteerism presents an essential component not just to the community's libraries but to the value of the community at large. In their publication *Managing Library Volunteers: A Practical Toolkit*, Driggers and Dumas remark on how volunteer opportunities enhance the democratic ideals of community participation and active involvement in local government. "Community participation in local libraries ensures that there will be a continuous flow of diverse ideas, skills, talents, and energies that will enable the library to continue to be a dynamic institution, a place where individuals and families choose to spend their time and give their support" (2002, p. 1). Serviceleader.org, a project of the RGK Center for Philanthropy and Community Service at the Lyndon B. Johnson School of Public Affairs at the University of Texas, Austin, emphasizes how organizations that value and employ the services of volunteers benefit in several ways while meeting the needs of the overall community. Volunteers endorse and support the organization publicly through the act of working alongside paid staff. As community representatives they can speak in favor of particular public policy at official meetings and through media editorials. Volunteers reach new audiences and work as unofficial ambassadors for new programs, recruit new monetary donations on the organization's behalf, and finally, when possible positions arise, cross over to become pre-oriented and experienced paid staff (Serviceleader.org 2003). Similarly, Annabel K. Stephens states in her recent article about the value of citizen participation in public libraries:

> people care more about institutions when they are given a chance to voice their opinions and to work for their benefit. They will become more aware of libraries' services and programs and thus more likely to use and publicize them. (Stephens 2003, p. 543)

Today's library volunteers fall under two distinct categories. The Friends of the Library, as previously discussed, operates as a separate organization with its own governing board and dues structure under the library's administrative umbrella. Principle goals are fundraising and political advocacy. The second category is that of general volunteers administered under the library's organization and coordination. General volunteers represent a wide intergenerational contingent of retired seniors, working and nonworking individuals, college students, and teen and high school members of the community. General volunteers contribute in a range of tasks, from book shelving to inventory assignments or tutoring in homework centers. Special projects such as book fairs or family and adult literacy programs often are successful due to the extraordinary amount of time volunteers donate, working with paid library staff to plan, implement, and evaluate these projects.

Creating a Volunteer Plan for Your SRP

Running a centers-based summer reading program requires the efforts of a group of volunteer workers joining forces with library youth staff for a smooth and effective operation. Providing meaningful responsibilities and expectations for your unpaid assistants is intrinsic to any successful volunteer initiative. In addition to satisfying personal motivation or need, most volunteers enjoy their assignments and are willing to continue to donate their time to the organization if they believe their efforts are accomplishing something worthwhile. This can only be achieved through careful consideration of how volunteers will fit into and enhance your entire program as you map out each portion of your summer's theme, center topics, and subthemes for each unit. Folding in volunteer hours into regularly scheduled story-hour sessions, book groups, and special events throughout the summer can also highlight where and how volunteers will make the difference for your summer plans.

Begin by creating a schedule of hours and tasks that you anticipate necessary to implement and maintain your programming.

- How many centers have you developed for the six-to-eight-week period?
- How much time will be needed to prepare each center with supplies and pre-arranged activity models?
- How much and what kind of help will you need for the open house and finale programs?
- How many volunteer hours will be necessary to add to staff hours for tidying up, restocking, maintaining, and supervising the exhibits on a daily basis?

Thinking about these and other questions should help you work out a detailed schedule of tasks and responsibilities to provide substantial assistance and a significant and rewarding volunteer experience for your potential SRP helpers. It also allows you to present a clear and feasible volunteer plan to a library administrator, volunteer

A Successful Volunteer Initiative

Provides Meaningful
   Responsibilities
   Expectations
   Choices

coordinator, or FOL board as part of your next step in promoting and recruiting your extra helping hands.

Important Things to Consider

While volunteers have been and are a continuing presence in libraries, there are some things to keep in mind before promoting and recruiting your SRP volunteer crew.

Does your library have a volunteer coordinator with established policies in place? It is important to find out information concerning policies related to insurance, liability, age requirements for minors, parental permission, and the like. Are your library employees under union contract and does recruiting volunteers for your specific program fall in violation of any contract regulations? How does your library cooperate with community service requirements from either the local school district or any church organizations? What, if any, relationship does your library have with local college and university education and library-science programs to provide opportunities for course-required field work? Meeting with your coordinator or administrator to answer and discuss these issues can help immensely with your initial planning as you become informed of existing policies and connections to help you recruit a crop of interested volunteers. It is also important to recognize that the volunteers you are seeking will be working directly with children and families and should be properly screened. Volunteer coordinators routinely interview prospective volunteers and even check up on references.

Your recreated summer reading program requires a specifically targeted group of interested assistants. Senior citizens and college students can provide some adult support and also offer an intergenerational facet to your program. Retired professionals can be trained as library docents to provide interactive exhibit support by working and reading with children at various centers. College education students seeking valuable experience interning with children often welcome the hands-on opportunities offered at your centers-based reading exhibits. High school students can also be a great boost to your program while earning valuable community service credits for graduation requirements. The Friends group may also provide a source of youthful assistance through a Teen Friends program. Teen Friends operate under the supervision of an adult leader yet function as an independent group with their own dues and organizational structure, choosing various projects and committees that benefit both young adult and youth services. A centers-based summer reading program can be a welcome project for this group to undertake.

Consider

Library policies for

    Insurance liability
    Age requirements
    Parental permission

Labor Union contracts

School or organization service credit requirements

Cooperation with

    University education and LIS programs

Screening of prospective volunteers

Once you have interviewed and selected your volunteer crew, orientation and training are essential in developing a group of capable and effective people to work with your program participants. An orientation meeting in the late spring can serve as a way to introduce your program's concept and interactive-centers model. Volunteers can be offered opportunities for planning and implementing, working directly with children throughout the summer, or both. Providing choice based on interest is another important aspect of successful volunteer initiatives.

The Benefits of Working with Tween Boosters

One of the best resources for volunteer help for the summer is to tap into your community's tween population. Middle-school students entering the sixth, seventh, and eighth grades make wonderful SRP volunteers or "tween boosters" and play a very important role in the overall summer program. In addition, including tween boosters allows both ends of the youth services target audience, from preschoolers through eighth graders, to be productively involved in summer library activities.

Today's tweens have been singled out by the advertising industry as a youth marketing bonanza. A revolutionized marketing strategy has had an enormous influence on tween behavior and parents and adults working with this age range have had to adapt. The service you provide to tweens today is directly affected by the niche advertising researchers and marketers have created to target a specific age group conditioned to behave more like adolescents than the children their chronological age indicates. And like it or not, libraries have been brought into this tween marketing frenzy.

Promoting summer reading to tweens must incorporate an aspect that appeals to the interests and abilities of older children who are not yet ready for the working world, but who can certainly contribute positively in ways that will bolster their self-esteem, responsibility, and altruism. Including tweens as part of your volunteer crew echoes a strong voice in character building, and further abets educational programs such as the nationally recognized Character Counts: Six Pillars of Character—trustworthiness, respect, responsibility, fairness, caring, and citizenship (Character Counts; http://www.charactercounts.org). Including children as volunteers "promotes healthy lifestyle and choices, enhances development, teaches life skills, improves the community, and encourages a lifelong service ethic" (Torres 2004). Youngsters in religious programs, scout troops, and other extracurricular commitments are often required to demonstrate volunteer service. Providing tweens meaningful volunteer opportunities, such as guiding younger children or working side-by-side with adults and professionals, can also be a first step on the long road to worthwhile paid employment. Over the last two decades, several libraries across the country have utilized tweens in summer reading volunteer roles with very positive results. In South Carolina, Leslie Barban, children's room manager at Richland County Public Library, reports on the successful four objectives of their 10-year Junior Volunteer Program that:

1. encourages children to become aware of and participate in activities offered by the library

2. emphasizes the value of contributing time, without remuneration, to a community agency
3. acquires volunteer help for accomplishing work of the library
4. enhances positive concepts and self-confidence while contributing as vital community members (Barban 1997, p. 94)

In Delmar, New York, Linda Massen at the Bethlehem Public Library refers to their two-decade middle-school volunteer program as a "hot ticket" family tradition. "Being a volunteer also leads to a reference for a first job, and kids learn about responsibility and gain the satisfaction of helping younger students improve their reading skills" (Massen 2003). In Colorado, Virginia Carlson at the Pikes Peak Library District engages youth volunteers as SRP registration greeters, craft and program assistants, and reading buddies. She reports the success of her volunteer program as a "significant contribution to the number of services and quality of customer service PPLD is able to provide. Indeed, teens are an energetic, motivated and talented human resource whose abilities can be marshaled in order to produce quality results and extend library resources" (Carlson 2003).

Generate Interest

Recruitment of a tween volunteer force begins in late spring with a direct campaign throughout the middle-school community and parent-teacher organizations. Different than the normal end-of-school-year library summer reading promotion, this campaign emphasizes the opportunities to

- earn service credit
- gain rewarding experience
- demonstrate talent and skills, and most important,
- have fun mentoring and working with younger children

Begin the campaign with a written open invitation to attend an early evening general organizational and informational meeting at which time specific roles, expectations from both sides, and sign-up contracts will be presented and explained. Include parents as well as tweens in the invitation. Involving parents establishes serious commitments and an overall understanding of the library's goals for an interactive centers-based summer reading program. A well-designed written invitation incorporates an energetic exciting statement; the date, time, and place of the meeting; a special activity for the evening; and of course the availability of food and treats.

Opening your tween volunteer opportunities to the entire middle-school community need not result in a chaotic descent of hundreds of students eager and willing to

A Well-Designed Invitation

Energetic, exciting statement
Date
Time
Place
Special activity
Food, treats, fun

participate. There will be those who attend the general meeting and realize a true commitment is not their partiality. From the hundred or so initial attendees at each of my yearly open meetings, roughly one quarter, or 25, tweens remained committed and returned with signed contracts and schedules for the summer period.

The organizational/informational meeting has two distinct purposes. Firstly, it gets everyone mingling a bit through a cooperative activity designed to relate to the summer theme chosen. This cooperative activity is meant to result in something useful and appropriate for the summer program and will demonstrate an immediate creative way your tweens' participation can have an important impact. You might have the tweens design welcome banners for the youth room, opening day bookmarks, or even their own SRP theme-related booster badges. While pizza, snacks, and drinks are passed around, explain the summer theme and how the idea of providing interactive exhibits will create a change of focus for the summer reading program. This is the time to instill a feeling of eagerness and welcomed participation. Find ways to tell

Handouts for Tween Boosters

Rights and Responsibilities
Job/Task List with descriptions
Contract

your tweens the merit their role as helpers and mentors plays and how the SRP activities *cannot* be successful without their assistance. The second purpose of the meeting is more serious and includes

- your explanation of the various jobs tweens may choose
- the expectations of the library youth staff
- the rights and responsibilities of tween volunteers
- the contract they will be expected to fill out and sign with a deadline date of return should they decide to join the library boosters program

It is advisable to NOT ask tweens to sign a contract the same evening of the open meeting. Allowing them a week to take the contract and task sheet home to evaluate with a parent helps them make a better-informed decision about their volunteer commitment. And with a week's grace period, you have a better chance of recruiting a group of truly interested tweens.

Like most children, tweens come with different levels of competencies, talents, and interests. Create volunteer opportunities that include a range of challenging yet workable duties and tasks. Write lists and explanations in a simple readable font with basic vocabulary easily understood by your prospective young volunteers.

The contract serves not only as a means to select specific jobs and hours while ensuring a commitment from a tween booster, but it also provides a liability disclaimer with a parental/legal guardian permission statement that must be completed with a signature. In addition, you will want to ask for information on the tween's possible summer out-of-town dates that will require rescheduling of volunteer hours in advance.

Orientation, Training, and Supervision

Your successful recruitment results in a core group of four to six general volunteers, perhaps including senior citizens, retired professionals, or college students, to commit to several hours per week with your program. Twenty to thirty tween boosters giving one to two hours per week fills out your volunteer schedule. Keep in mind that tweens want to balance their volunteer schedule with other summer scheduling of day camp, family vacations, and possible school or enrichment classes. Both your core group of volunteers and your tween boosters can be brought together for training and a get-acquainted session prior to the summer reading program's opening event. Instill an atmosphere of mutual respect and camaraderie with an opening icebreaker. A getting-to-know-everyone activity such as a name crostics puzzle will do nicely. Provide a tour of the youth library and how the room will be transformed for the theme and exhibit centers. Indicate how supplies are to be stored and doled out as centers are used. Review

Tween Booster's Rights and Responsibilities

Rights

- The right to a clear job/task description
- The right to receive adequate training for the job or task chosen
- The right to be treated with respect and courtesy by library staff
- The right to voice concerns or grievances to a supervisor
- The right to be involved with his/her evaluation
- The right to be recognized for volunteer efforts contributing to a successful job or library project

Responsibilities

- To accept an assignment after thoughtful consideration
- To report to your work station on time
- To fulfill your commitment or notify your supervisor in a timely manner
- To adhere to the guidelines of the library's code of dress, decorum, and work ethic
- To be considerate and respectful of both library patrons and staff
- To provide honest feedback and suggestions to library staff

The Library's Responsibilities to Tween Boosters

- To provide a safe and respectful working environment
- To provide appropriate information and training for the job/task
- To provide effective feedback on work and duties performed
- To officially recognize a Booster's contribution in time, talent, and skill

Adapted from Preston Driggers and Eileen Dumas, *Managing Library Volunteers: A Practical Toolkit* (Chicago: American Library Association, 2002), p. 18, and Dale Freund, "Do Volunteers Belong in the Library?" *Rural Libraries* 25, no. 1 (2005): p. 26.

Summer Reading Program
Tween Booster Job/Task List

Open House Kick-Off Program

1. Set-Up Crew—Assist in preparation of Open House decorations, activity center units, and game areas
2. Registration Assistant—help staff table, explain program, pass out sign-up forms and welcome packet
3. Interactive Center Docent—help participants understand concept and work with particular activity or project
4. Craft Table Assistant—help with specific craft design, maintain supplies in order
5. Game Monitor—help supervise game table or section
6. Clean-Up crew—assist in tearing down community room open house setup

Story Hour Buddy

1. Assist librarian in story-hour session with music and craft activity
2. Assist in providing positive role modeling for young story listeners

Interactive Center Docent

1. Help participants understand concept and work with particular activity or project
2. Clean up center and restock materials

Interactive Center Reading or Web Site Buddy

1. Read assigned book at center with or to participating child
2. Assist child in exploring assigned Web site for center activity

Special Events Host Assistant

1. Help seat and monitor children as needed

Book Group Hospitality Assistant

1. Help with snacks and/or serving of food

Shelving Assistant

1. Sort and prepare book carts for shelving

Summer Reading Finale Program Host

1. Assist with seating and monitoring of attendees
2. Assist with passing out of completed certificates
3. Host and monitor snack/food table

Summer Reading Program
Tween Booster Application/Contract

Name: _____ Age: _____ (11-14)

Address: _____

City: _____ Zip: _____

Home Phone: _____ Emergency Contact & Phone: _____

BOOSTER OPPORTUNITIES	TASKS	MEETS — WHEN (CIRCLE THE DATE/TIME YOU ARE AVAILABLE)	DATES/TIMES ASSIGNED (YOUTH STAFF WILL FILL IN)
Open House Kick-Off Program	Set-Up Crew Registration Assistant Craft Table Assistant Interactive Center Docent Games Monitor Clean-Up Crew	Monday, June 18 1:30 - 2:30 p.m. 2:30 - 3:30 p.m. 3:30 - 4:30 p.m. 4:30 - 5:30 p.m.	
Story Hour Buddy (No more than 2 assigned at one story hour.)	Help out in story hour and craft	Tuesday or Thursday 9:15 - 10:15 a.m. 1:45 - 2:45 p.m.	
Interactive Center Docent (2 hour per day maximum)	1. Preparing and stocking supplies 2. Assisting with center projects	Your choice of day: _____ Your choice of day: _____	
Reading Buddy	Read with or to a child at center		
Website Buddy	Guide child or family at center		
Special Event Host Assistant (No more than 4 assigned to one show.)	Seat & Monitor Program	June 27 - 7 p.m.	
Traveling Theatre Host Assistant (No more than 4 assigned to one show.)	Seat & Monitor Program	July 18 - 11 a.m. or 2 p.m.	
Book Group Hospitality Assistant (No more than 4 assigned to one show.)	Seat & Monitor Program	August 1 - 7 p.m.	
Finale Program Host Assistant (No more than 4 assigned to one show.)	Seat & Monitor Program Pass out certificates Host snack/food table	Wednesday, August 8 7 p.m.	
Shelving Assistant	Sort and prepare book carts	Your choice of day and time: _____	

Will you be going away this summer? Yes_____ No _____ If so, when? _____

Parent/Legal Guardian's Permission:

_____ has my permission to work as a Tween Booster Volunteer at _____ Library.

Parent/Legal Guardian's Signature: _____

Parent/Legan Guardian's Phone When Tween is at Library: _____ Date: _____

Return completed application/contract with signed parental/legal guardian permission to the library youth desk.

From *Summer Reading Renaissance: An Interactive Exhibits Approach* by Rita Soltan. Illustrations by Jill Reichenbach Fill. Westport, CT: Libraries Unlimited. Copyright © 2008.

how the philosophy behind your newly created centers-based summer reading program is dependent on their devoted help. Go over specific jobs/tasks with explanations and perhaps model some of the exhibit projects. Invite parents of tween boosters to attend this meeting as well.

Name Crostics Puzzle

Write your name on an index card
Circulate throughout the group
How many names can you attach to your own name?

    JENNY
    A
    SARAH
    O
    NANCY
        E
        D

Parents need to be included in the expectations of the library's volunteer program and are instrumental in ensuring its success. Parental attendance provides "opportunities to express any concern or ask questions . . . being fully informed makes it easier for the parent to sign the permission notice. This also guarantees that the child will attend the training or orientation since the parent will also be there" (Torres 2004).

One of the benefits of having a volunteer crew that encompasses an intergenerational range of people is that you may develop teams to work together by pairing a couple of children with an older volunteer. "Non-related intergenerational teams of children paired with adolescents or senior citizens to complete a volunteer assignment is useful to maximize child supervision, while allowing equal contribution" (Ellis 2003). These teams allow for more efficient participation under a watchful eye from the youth staff.

Like a Paid Position

Supervision of all volunteers is a necessity in that it provides feedback and support to your volunteers, as well as a means to oversee your program is being well served. All volunteers need to know who their immediate staff contact is and should feel free to communicate both concerns and suggestions.

The significance of individual evaluations for all volunteers is equal to that of any job performance review. Continued observation by library staff, coupled with honest feedback and positive acknowledgement, invokes a mindset of worthwhile accomplishment while providing additional training when needed. With tweens as well as older volunteers, if a particular assignment is not quite working out, the evaluation period is a way to alter the situation to a more positive scenario. Evaluation also provides tweens with an understanding of the importance of good work and genuine job performance expectations, which can lead to good recommendations for future positions or placements. A proper evaluation works as a genuine two-way conversation and discussion, at which time both staff supervisor and volunteer may be able to voice positive commentary as well as areas of concern. Some libraries offer official written evaluation forms. For tweens, a simple summarized paragraph of the evaluative discussion may be more efficient and effective. The written summary can also serve as

Tween Booster Evaluation Form

Booster's Name:

Job Assignments:

The Youth Staff would like your thoughts on your volunteer experience this summer.

Things I especially enjoyed about being a library Tween Booster:

Suggestions for making the Tween Booster program better:

Supervisor's Comments:

Proclamation Declaring Tween Booster Recognition
Summer Reading Program Finale

Whereas, _____ Library Tween Boosters
Library Name
are between the ages of 11 and 14 and work alongside our general
volunteers, Friends of the Library, and Library staff,

and

Whereas, _____ Tween Boosters gave their time
# of Tweens
to assist in the _____ Library Summer Reading Program
Library Name
contributing _____ volunteer hours this summer,
# of Hours

and

Whereas, _____ Library Tween Boosters
Library Name
mentored and assisted children and families at our SRP exhibits,
interactive centers, story hours, and other programs,

and

Whereas, _____ Library Tween Boosters
Library Name
contributed to the overall goals of providing
an educational summer enrichment program
within a recreational and informal, free-choice
learning environment,

I, _____, now therefore formally
Library Director or Town Official
recognize and thank
List Tween Volunteers by Name Here

for their individual contribution and participation in
_____ Library Summer Reading Tween Booster Program.
Library Name

Tween Boosters Time Sheet

Date	Time In	Booster or Volunteer	Job/Task/Assignment	Time Out	Total Time

a formal recommendation for future volunteer placement. Regardless of the method, make time for evaluations within the first month, so that a whole summer does not go by with poor or unacceptable performance results hampering your program.

Thank Yous and Acknowledgments

Recognition of all volunteers requires continual consistent praise and acknowledgment coupled with formal ceremonial appreciation for dedicated, good service. Thanking your volunteers daily as they sign in and out, perform their responsibilities, deal with little issues or problems, and generally hold down the fort while you undertake other larger obligations instills confidence and self-worth in your younger and older volunteers. Beyond the daily thank you, including your tweens in any of the volunteer recognition programs routinely offered on a yearly basis at your library, such as a volunteer appreciation tea or a community-wide volunteer recognition day, allows tweens to feel equally appreciated with their older volunteer counterparts. Another way to make your tweens feel especially appreciated is to declare a portion of the summer reading finale program for tween booster appreciation. Invite your library director or an official from your community to read aloud a "proclamation" you have written that lists all the ways your tween boosters' participation made the summer reading program a success. Each tween can be named individually and presented with a special recognition ribbon or certificate. Nominations for special volunteer service awards throughout your community or school district are other ways to offer recognition to your hard-working, dedicated group of young volunteers. Ultimately, your successful volunteer recruitment, training, supervision, and recognition play an important role in the development of your tween boosters' maturity and encouragement of lifelong altruistic service while providing the essential extra to complete your centers-based summer reading program.

References

Barban, Leslie. 1997. "Building Character and Responsibility: A Decade of Junior Volunteers." *American Libraries* (June/July): 94–96.

Carlson, Virginia. 2003. "Summer Teen Volunteers at Pikes Peak Library District." *Colorado Libraries*, 29, no. 3 (Fall).

Character Counts: Six Pillars of Character. http://www.josephsoninstitute.org/MED/MED-2 sixpillars.htm (accessed September 9, 2007).

Driggers, Preston, and Eileen Dumas. 2002. *Managing Library Volunteers: A Practical Toolkit.* Chicago: American Library Association.

Ellis, Susan J. "Why Volunteer?" http://www.serviceleader.org/new/volunteers/articles/ 2003/04/000048.php (accessed August 17, 2004).

Ellis, Susan J. 2003. "Children Should Be Seen and Heard—As Volunteers." *Voluntary Action Leadership Journal* (Summer): 24–28, quoted in Gabina Torres, "The Future of Volunteering: Children under the Age of 14 as Volunteers," p. 10–11. http://www.serviceleader. org/new/managers/2004/06/000244.php (accessed September 8, 2007).

Massen, Linda. 2003. "A Hot Ticket: Middle Schoolers Can't Resist Our Summer-Reading Program." *School Library Journal.* http://www.schoollibraryjournal.com/article/CA294419. html?q=hot+ticket (accessed August 30, 2007).

Poplau, Ronald W. *The Doer of Good Becomes Good: A Primer on Volunteerism.* Lanham, Maryland: Scarecrow Education, 2004.

Serviceleader.org. 2003. "Why Involve Volunteers?" http://www.serviceleader.org/new/managers/2003/04/000063.php (retrieved August 17, 2004).

Stephens, Annabel K. 2003. "Citizen Participation in Libraries." *Encyclopedia of Library and Information Science* (June): 543, quoted in Dale Freund, "Do Volunteers Belong in the Library?" *Rural Libraries* 25, no. 1 (2005): 34.

Torres, Gabina. 2004. "The Future of Volunteering: Children under the Age of 14 as Volunteers." http://www.serviceleader.org/new/managers/2004/06/000244.php (accessed September 8, 2007).

Wyly, Mary. 1992. "Uncommon Human Resources: The Newberry Library Volunteer Program." *Library Trends* 41, no. 2 (Fall): 316(14). Academic OneFile (accessed August 18, 2007).

5

Review and Reflect: Measuring Outcomes

An effective and content-rich centers-based summer reading program can only be complete with a planned formal evaluation procedure. Children's and youth services librarians tend to instinctively interpret results of their well-intended hard work when a story-hour group displays gleeful joy at the reading of a funny or absurd picture book or children leave a craft- or art-based program proudly carrying their newest creation. While systematically recording attendance numbers on monthly statistical reports indicates a quantitative degree of success, it is our patrons' level of pleasure, satisfaction, and fulfillment we continually infer and monitor to provide us with a kind of qualitative sense of accomplishment and achievement. Intuitively, we know that our programs foster early literacy skills, engage parents and children in reading-together activities, and inspire life-long reading interest and enjoyment. Validating our instincts, thoughts, and feelings concerning the success of our programs in quantitative terms with hard evidence is another matter.

In recent years the traditional methods of gathering and recording data for evaluation depended solely on the counting of the "input," or resources available, and the "output," or products delivered. Filling up those monthly, semiannual, and annual reports with numbers has been standard to indicate:

- library building usage by children and families based on head counts
- youth materials used based on circulation and turn-over figures
- availability of resources based on interloan and fill-rate statistics
- reference services based on transaction counts
- use of programming based on attendance figures
- public and community outreach based on school, day-care, and community center visits in and outside the library

Accountability and justifiable requests for higher budgets and more staff hours have placed librarians in a position to answer to administrators and government officials with quantifiable results. All this counting leads to analysis and comparison of previous years, where percentage increases or decreases in data based on categories can either further a program idea or squash it. We are reminded by managers that this sort of data-gathering measurement is a way to interpret whether or not we are achieving the goals we have assigned for the services we provide. However, as Virginia Walter states in her 1992 publication, "for the most part the output measures only tell you 'how many' of something in relation to 'how many' of something else. They don't tell you 'why' or 'how' or 'so what' " (Walter 1992, p. 19).

Evaluation is much more than counting and interpreting figures. Evaluation requires careful appraisal and study of what we do and how our work is received by the children and families we serve. What specific difference do our programs make and what is the best way to document this difference beyond quantitative statistics gathered through recording the number of children registered, number of books read, number of program attendees, and even number of centers completed? As Peggy Rudd, Director-Librarian for the Texas State Library and Archives Commission, notes in her introductory IMLS grant evaluation paper, verifying our intuition that libraries and programs have a profound impact on individuals, institutions, and communities must be done by devising a system that measures outcomes (Rudd 1999).

Evaluating the quality of the work we do as children's librarians is being recognized more these days in suggested methods of outcome measures. "Outcome measures indicate the impact or effects of the public library and its information services on a specific individual and the surrounding community" (Matthews 2004, p. 3). We must consider ways to measure the quality of a summer reading centers-based program using indicators or data that will tell us

- the program's influence on children's reading interests, stability, and progress
- the program's results on narrowing summer reading loss
- the importance of using centers and informal learning activities
- the benefits to participants' experiences within the three contexts of an informal learning environment—personal context, socio-cultural context, physical context

This type of qualitative measurement is less tangible yet increasingly important as librarians are learning to focus evaluation more on the social, educational, and recreational difference the public library and its programming can make within the community. Creating a method for this kind of qualitative or outcome measurement requires careful deliberation on why this particular kind of evaluation is necessary and useful.

Analyzing a summer reading program through qualitative or outcome measurement allows you to view results from the perspective of your patrons and program participants, thereby making you more aware of *their* particular interests and needs. As the program progresses, observation and monitoring can help you document any unforeseen developments, both positive and negative. Recording what went right or wrong, what could be enhanced, eliminated, altered, or left the same, allows you to reflect on improvement and the program's limitations based on characteristics identified from the users' perspectives. How well you achieve the goals you design allows you to interpret the impact the program has had on participants in the library or in the community at-large. This type of analysis has been outlined in the publication *Taking Stock: A Practical Guide to Evaluating Your Own Programs*. The authors make a distinction between formative evaluation and summative evaluation, noting that "formative evaluation provides information as a program takes form while monitoring progress as programs are occurring and summative evaluation occurs when you are summing up what you have achieved" (Bond, Boyd, and Rapp 1997, p. 6–7). This type of summative evaluation is structured around four separate yet connected processes:

- Framing the Evaluation—identify needs, document context and available resources, design strategies
- Defining Goals and Objectives—consistent with needs, generate questions, select indicators and outcomes
- Finding Evidence—through records and documents, observation, interviews, surveys
- Making Sense of the Evidence—look for themes, interpret data, report results (Bond, Boyd, and Rapp 1997, p. 2)

More recently, outcome-based evaluation has been developed and modeled by the United Way of America to provide agencies receiving United Way funding with a uniform mechanism to comply with outcome measures. This outcome-based evaluation offers a logical addition to an existing quantitative evaluation process combining quantitative data with qualitative information. The "Logic Model" for outcome-based measurement, developed by the United Way of America and adapted for its grants programming by the Institute of Museum and Library Services, incorporates four basic components:

- Inputs—resources dedicated to or consumed by a program
- Activities—what the program does with the inputs to fulfill its mission
- Outputs—direct products of program activities (number of attendees, etc.)
- Outcomes—benefits or changes for individuals or populations during or after participation (Rudd 1999, p. 20)

The first three of these components fall under a quantitative evaluation, while the last is the process by which qualitative evaluation may be obtained. The Logic Model for defining and measuring outcomes developed by IMLS follows a basic plan that demonstrates

- how outcomes will be measured
- how certain information will be collected
- from whom information will be collected
- when information will be collected
- what target goals have been chosen for the defined outcomes (Motylewski 2002)

Authors Dresang, Gross, and Holt (2006) take the concept of outcome-based evaluation one step further by suggesting another model—"outcome-based planning and evaluation." A key element to their model is the inclusion of the planning process. "Planning and evaluation are inseparable, with the planning process incorporating iterative evaluation. Planning is not finished at any one point in time but rather is ongoing and continually influenced and modified by the frequent evaluation activities" (Dresang, Gross, and Holt 2006, p. 11). As your summer reading centers-based program is developed and

Outcome Data Gathering

Informal interviews
Surveys
Focus groups
Staff observations
Staff logs

then carried out, determining how participants will react—by their change in behavior, the addition of a skill or extension of prior knowledge, their connection in a personal or social context, and the formation of a new understanding of their surrounding world—will lead to evaluation of how and if these outcomes actually came about, which in turn will influence further planning and implementation of each subsequent program.

In all of these models, outcomes may be measured through a variety of methods that can be effective in documenting and outlining your program's specific success, effectiveness, and value to its constituents. Methods may include informal interviews, surveys, focus groups, and the logging of staff observations.

Informal interviews are one of the most personal ways of gaining insight into how children and families are reacting to your program. Conversation is a natural part of every children's librarian's role at the reference or summer reading check-in desk as families approach for guidance on book selection, game-sheet stamping, and lotto entries. You may spark a child or parent or both to present you with some quick feedback when you greet a child and admire a completed project done at a center, or you may simply initiate a response by asking

> "Did you have fun today?" "What did you like about your time at the library today?"
> "What did you do at the interactive centers area?"
> "What story did you read or game did you play?"

If appropriate you might then continue with a simple, "What else would you have liked to do?" While this sort of interview and response may seem haphazard, you may find that as you talk with your patrons over a month or two, a pattern of responses both positive and negative will emerge to bring out information on the program's attributes and fallbacks.

A reference desk log is another way to record requests and feedback for a variety of services. A standard way of documenting collection development needs is by maintaining a log of reference questions submitted by subject area and school-based assignments. Similarly, staff may keep a summer reading journal or log recording comments and requests that families present. In addition, as staff members keep watchful eyes over the room, the library collection, traffic patterns, and interactive-center usage, the recording of their observations is another useful tool to employ.

A thoughtful and carefully constructed survey that is simple and quick to fill out can provide a snapshot picture of how your patrons received and interpreted your program and the interactive exhibits you designed. For adults, a multiple choice–style of about 10 questions, with additional opportunity to include suggestions or recommendations, is useful, while children will need something written in a simple, easy-to-understand language in which they can respond affirmatively or negatively. Employing a graphic mechanism allows the youngest or the less literate to participate and provide feedback. Both surveys can be kept at the desk during the last two weeks and handed out with lotto entries and game-sheet stamps. Patrons can also be encouraged to complete the surveys at the centers area.

A focus group may be another way to instigate a more detailed interpretation of your program through a carefully facilitated discussion meeting where answers and comments to open-ended questions are written and summarized by a recorder. You might want to invite participants from several venues offered throughout the summer, including parents who attend your story hours, book discussions, visit regularly with their child, or come in purely to use and check out the collection. You may wish to include both children and adults at a meeting or divide the groups. The questions you develop for this meeting can hopefully trigger an exchange of worthwhile ideas and commentary as you encourage your focus group to feel comfortable in their participation. A good 30-to-40-minute discussion from a representative group of summer reading families and children can provide you with some essential and critical information. It should be noted that requesting feedback from nonparticipating families, through a survey or a focus group, will also give you insight from the other perspective and may provide valuable data on what can be changed or added to recruit new families and children in the future.

Acquiring information in these four ways opens up an issue of ethics and privacy. Anonymity is an essential component and must be stressed both in the information-gathering techniques and in the subsequent reports compiled. Assuring your participants of this factor and eliminating specific names and identifying information is crucial to engaging their voluntary cooperation with your evaluation procedures.

These methods of acquiring outcome information are a form of research not without its limitations. Outcome-based evaluation is not and should not be equated with formal research that attempts to compare data and methodology for similar studies. "As a management tool it [outcome-based evaluation] may suggest cause and effect but it does not try to prove it" (Association of Children's Museums 2003). The mere informality and somewhat random collection of data of the above-described methods cannot possibly provide foolproof evidence, but rather can generate what researchers deem "good enough" data that when analyzed produces "useful and credible" information (Hernon 2002, p. 99). The information gathered will review how your program affected or changed your community's summer reading attitudes, behavior, reasons for visiting the library, and participating in the program. The information will also indicate whether or not the goals you originally outlined were met and help you communicate your program's overall value to your stakeholders and constituents.

Let us look more closely at an outcome-based evaluation plan for a summer reading program designed around interactive exhibits and centers.

Purpose of SRP

To provide a venue to encourage continued summertime reading within a structured, theme-based, informal learning environment.

Program Services

- Game sheets and completion certificates
- Weekly interactive exhibits and centers employing games, puzzles, art, math, science, technology, and literature
- Trained assistance from library staff and volunteers
- Story hours, book discussions, special events, and performances

Intended Outcomes

1. Children and families will experience multiple library visits within three contexts of an informal learning environment.

   - Personal Context—an affective experience gained through the free-choice of working at a variety of centers offering content-rich, intriguing, creative, and unique concepts.
   - Socio-Cultural Context—a convivial and communal experience gained by group participation at the centers with friends and family and attendance at programs or events.
   - Physical Context—a greater awareness gained of the library's collection of materials, objects, and books as combined with center concepts and themes.

2. Children and families will continue to read alone or with a parent or family member several times per week throughout the summer.

Indicators

- # of families who visited library at least 2 times per week
- # of families who reported working on centers
- # of families who reported attending a program
- # of families who gained new experience at centers
- # of families who read something related to theme and center topics
- # of families who reported reading at home

Data Sources

Informal interviews
Staff log entries
Participant survey
Focus groups

Target for Outcomes

The goal is that 85 percent of families visiting the library during the summer will include the exhibits and centers as an additional informal learning resource to encourage continued interest and progress in their child's summertime reading.

Sample Family Survey

Your family's participation in the Summer Reading Program (SRP) is very important. We welcome your feedback on how the program contributed to your child's summertime reading.

Number of children in SRP _____

Ages of children in SRP _____

Please check all that apply:

1. We learned about the SRP

   a. At school _____
   b. At the library _____
   c. From a friend _____
   d. From the media _____

2. We enjoyed coming to the library this summer to

   a. Check out books _____
   b. Work at an interactive exhibit center _____
   c. Attend a program _____
   d. Other _____

3. The interactive exhibit centers

   a. Introduced us to new ideas _____
   b. Helped us meet new people _____
   c. Presented new reading choices _____
   d. Were not part of our visits _____

4. The content and design of the interactive exhibit centers were

   a. Too challenging for my child _____
   b. Appropriate for my child with some volunteer or adult assistance _____
   c. Not challenging enough for my child _____
   d. Did not apply to my child _____

5. How much did the interactive exhibit centers add to your child's and family's summer reading experience?

   a. Very much _____
   b. Some _____
   c. Not much _____
   d. Not at all _____

6. We visited the library this summer

   a. 1 time per week _____
   b. 2 times per week _____
   c. More than 2 times per week _____

From *Summer Reading Renaissance: An Interactive Exhibits Approach* by Rita Soltan. Illustrations by Jill Reichenbach Fill. Westport, CT: Libraries Unlimited. Copyright © 2008.

7. We read together or alone

   a. Every day _____
   b. Once or twice per week _____
   c. Only at the library _____

8. This summer our participation helped my child to

   a. Enjoy reading
      more _____
      same _____
      less _____
   b. Increase reading skill _____
   c. Discover new topics _____
   d. Create and learn through art, science, technology, and writing _____

9. Our favorite part of the summer reading program was _____

10. The part of the summer reading program we liked least was _____

    Suggestions or recommendations _____

From *Summer Reading Renaissance: An Interactive Exhibits Approach* by Rita Soltan. Illustrations by Jill Reichenbach Fill. Westport, CT: Libraries Unlimited. Copyright © 2008.

Sample Child Survey

I am a BOY or GIRL

I am going into _____ grade in the fall.

Please Draw a Happy or Sad Face After Each Question

1. I like visiting the library.

2. I like the summer reading program at the library.

3. I like to read by myself.

4. I like to take books home to read.

5. I like to read with someone or when someone reads aloud to me.

6. The summer reading program helps me read better.

7. The projects and games are interesting and fun to do.

8. The projects and games help me learn new things.

9. I made new friends at the library.

10. I like to read just for fun every day.

From *Summer Reading Renaissance: An Interactive Exhibits Approach* by Rita Soltan. Illustrations by Jill Reichenbach Fill. Westport, CT: Libraries Unlimited. Copyright © 2008.

Sample Focus Group Questions or Prompts

1. How do you use the library with your family or child?
2. What did the summer reading program add to your weekly routine with your family?
3. How did working or participating at the interactive exhibit centers add or detract from your library visits?
4. What new ideas, concepts, or topics did you gain or learn about at the interactive exhibit centers?
5. Did the centers inspire you to look for and check out books on new topics?
6. What did you like about the interactive exhibit centers?
7. What did you think about the help the Tween Boosters and volunteers provided at the centers?
8. What would you recommend we add, leave alone, or change for a future similarly designed summer reading centers-based program?

Since your newly revised and recreated summer reading program depends, in part, on the voluntary efforts of the older children recruited for the Tween Boosters Volunteer Program, it is similarly important to include an outcome-based assessment for this significant portion of the program as part of your overall evaluation. An outcome-based evaluation plan for a Tween Boosters Volunteer Program could include the following:

Purpose of the Tween Boosters Volunteer Program

Children between the ages of 11–14 will have the opportunity to participate in a summer reading program as volunteer assistants to the library staff, children, and families.

Program Services

Invitational recruitment meeting
Orientation and training
Ongoing feedback, support, and guidance from library staff
Service credit cooperation with school or community organization

Intended Outcomes

1. Tweens, children ages 11–14, will gain an appreciation for volunteer work.
2. Tweens, children ages 11–14, will gain experience in a work environment.
3. Tweens, children ages 11–14, will gain a sense of positive personal attributes including higher self-esteem, responsibility, and respect.
4. Tweens, children ages 11–14, will use the library for their own reading interests with a greater sense of confidence and knowledge.

Indicators

of tweens who reported learning from the volunteer experience
# of tweens who reported feeling positive about their volunteer experience
# of tweens who reported reading during the summer
# of tweens who reported having more confidence in using the library
# of tweens who reported would return and volunteer again

Target for Outcomes

The goal is that 95 percent of the Tween Booster volunteers will have consistently kept their commitment throughout the program and expressed a sense of satisfaction in their volunteer efforts.

In addition to the survey, personal interviews at performance-evaluation time and a final general meeting or focus group with your tweens may present other opportunities for information gathering.

Once your outcome-based evaluation is complete, your final evaluation report will incorporate both the quantitative data as traditionally gathered with the new qualitative information you have compiled. Results will hopefully lead you to a better

Sample Survey for Tween Boosters

We thank you for your volunteer commitment this summer and want to know your thoughts.

I am a BOY _____ GIRL _____

I am going into _____ grade

Please check all that apply:

1. I found out about the Tween Boosters Volunteer Program

    a. At school _____
    b. At the library _____
    c. From an invitational postcard _____
    d. Other _____

2. At the invitational open house I learned

    a. What a Tween Booster volunteer can do _____
    b. What the Summer Reading Program is about _____
    c. How I can help the library staff _____
    d. How I can help the younger children in the program _____
    e. About my "Rights and Responsibilities" as a Tween Booster _____
    f. About the various jobs or assignments I may choose _____

3. I found my responsibilities to be

    a. Challenging _____
    b. Uninteresting _____
    c. Helpful to others _____
    d. Satisfying _____

4. The Tween Booster Volunteer Program encouraged me to

    a. Become more responsible _____
    b. Understand my role as a volunteer _____
    c. Use the library more confidently _____

5. This summer I read

    More _____
    Same _____
    Less _____

6. Please let us know what you enjoyed or did not enjoy about the program

    I enjoyed

    I did not enjoy

7. I would like to come back as a Tween Booster next summer

    a. Yes _____
    b. No _____

From *Summer Reading Renaissance: An Interactive Exhibits Approach* by Rita Soltan. Illustrations by Jill Reichenbach Fill. Westport, CT: Libraries Unlimited. Copyright © 2008.

understanding of the successes and shortcomings of your program and to the planning phase of next year's theme with a renewed energy for developing a summer reading program into a content-rich and rewarding experience for your community, families, and children.

References

Association of Children's Museums. 2003. *Knowing What Audiences Learn: Outcomes and Program Planning.* Washington, DC: Institute of Museum and Library Services. http://www.imls.gov/ppt/ACM-03-fnl.pps (accessed September 26, 2007).

Bond, Sally, Sally E. Boyd, and Kathleen A. Rapp. 1997. *Taking Stock: A Practical Guide to Evaluating Your Own Programs.* Chapel Hill, NC: Horizon Research Inc.

Dresang, Eliza T., Melissa Gross, and Leslie Edmonds, Holty. 2006. *Dynamic Youth Services Through Outcome-Based Planning and Evaluation.* Chicago: American Library Association.

Hernon, Peter, and Robert E. Dugan. 2002. *An Action Plan for Outcomes Assessment in Your Library.* Chicago: American Library Association.

Matthews, Joseph R. 2004. *Measuring for Results: The Dimensions of Public Library Effectiveness.* Westport, CT: Libraries Unlimited.

Motylewski, K., and C. Horn. 2002. *IMLS Grant Applicants Outcome Based Evaluation Frequently Asked Questions.* http://www.imls.gov/applicants/faqs.shtm (accessed September 26, 2007).

Powell, Ronald R. 2006. "Evaluation Research: An Overview." *Library Trends* 55 (1): 2006, pp. 102–20.

Rudd, Peggy D. 1999. "Documenting the Difference: Demonstrating the Value of Libraries Through Outcome Measurement." In *Perspectives on Outcome Based Evaluation for Libraries and Museums.* Washington, DC: Institute of Museum and Library Services, pp. 16–22. http://www.imls.gov/pdf/pubobe.pdf (accessed September 22, 2007).

Walter, Virginia A. 1992. *Output Measures for Public Library Service to Children: A Manual of Standardized Procedures.* Chicago: American Library Association.

Part 2

Sample Centers-Based Programs

6

Interactive Intrigue

Summer reading program themes have traditionally been chosen for their universal child appeal, enticing kids to sign up early in the season and return to the library often for those incremental incentives. Generic themes such as "Splish, Splash, Read," "Reading Rocks," or "Step to the Beat . . . Read" are meant to be great cheering slogans for summer programs that follow a numbers course of counting hours or books for a final overall preset reading goal. A centers-based program requires choosing themes that lend themselves to enough content and development so children and families will be encouraged to return on their own, discover, create, and of course read with the exhibits you provide.

The themes and center content outlined in the following chapters follow a simple organizational approach. The time span of your program, together with the location and size of your exhibit/centers area, are the first things to consider as you begin to decide how to divide and build the theme into manageable subthemes and interactive-learning centers. For example, with the Australian "Summer Down Under" theme, I looked at the typical time span of an SRP running seven to eight weeks throughout the months of mid-June to mid-August. I then explored the country of Australia through my collection and the Internet. This type of research need not take weeks. A few hours of reading and outlining key areas of the subject that you feel will be stimulating, engaging, and overall inviting to children's general curiosity are the subthemes you are looking to define. I decided to create four subthemes over the seven-or-eight-week period that would introduce the country of Australia and then delve into some of the features to offer an "Aussie Experience" without actually traveling to the continent. My outline incorporated some general Australia specifics, a focus on the Aboriginal society, and part of Australia's historical aspects organized into two-week segments as follows:

Sample Preliminary Outline for Interactive Centers for
Summer Down Under: An Awesome Aussie Experience

Weeks 1 & 2—The Lucky Country, Australia
1. Get to know the country known as Oz (national symbols, etc.)
2. Australia's slang language
3. Geography

4. Cuisine
5. Geology and climate

Weeks 3 & 4—Walkabout the Outback
1. Wildlife and plants
2. Great Barrier Reef
3. Aboriginal people/society

Weeks 5 & 6—Dreamtime: The Aboriginal Arts
1. Music
2. Art
3. Storytelling

Weeks 7 & 8—Back in Time with Australia's Fascinating History
1. Historical timeline
2. Exploration of Australia
3. Penal colony and Britain
4. Noteworthy Australians

Now the work of creating a variety of interactive exhibits with games, art projects, puzzles, and simple applications could begin. I kept in mind certain overall principles before I could develop my centers.

I considered the location and size of my exhibit/center area and how many interactive centers I could feasibly offer simultaneously within one subtheme. Realistically you need not offer more than two. Three or four can make even a large area crowded, especially if several families participate at the same time. Planning a subtheme over a two-week period allows for centers to be extended and gives the added plus of changing your exhibits weekly so that families can anticipate and visit your library more often. In the "Invention Convention" theme, three different activities extend the concept of the use of numbers and counting through a magic squares sheet, the application of an abacus, and finally the playing of the mancala game. These three activities can be laid out in one center for a week's period or held over for an additional week if you choose to extend the theme's first unit. My youth room was divided into three basic sections—a preschool floor play area, a sitting/reading/study area with only two large tables seating 12, and a shelving area with a collection of at least 65,000 items. I decided to create a U-shaped seating area by adding one folding table to the existing furniture, thereby increasing the seating capacity to 24–30 with people sitting on both sides (see floor plan in chapter 3 figure 3.1).

When developing specific activities, incorporating a variety of methods that lend themselves to some perceptive understanding is better than just applying an arts and crafts project. Arts and crafts are great fun, but remember to use them in a way that contributes to some aspect of the purpose of the theme or concepts you are displaying. Simple experiments connected to a story or book on display, such as the one demonstrating the seesaw-lever concept in the industrial technology unit of "Invention Convention," avoid crafts altogether. However, in the same theme, having children reproduce Ben Franklin's kite and key from a template will also work to get the point of his experiment across. Try out and test all the displays and interactive activities ahead to see how long it will take the average child and parent to complete, how well your directions apply, and how your supplies will pan out. Clearly print and mount demonstration

Try Out and Test Activities for

Average time-span
Direction application
Supply usage

explanations and directions at the center with samples for each activity. And remember, assistance and modeling from your boosters and volunteers will always be appreciated.

Making use of computers, and especially the Internet, can enhance your exhibits in a way that requires less preparation by you and, for participants, more visual and auditory exposure to a concept. The sample plans include numerous suggestions for related Internet sites that can be featured as part of a center through a computer station specifically designated for this purpose. Allowing kids to take a virtual tour of Captain Cook's ship, the *Endeavor*, or the International Space Station through Web sites maintained by the National Library of Australia and Discover.com respectively are examples of how the use of the Internet can sometimes be more effective and interesting. And as with any other Web site recommendation that you might include in your everyday collection development, apply the same rules of appropriate content without commercial interference through advertising. Please note that all Web site addresses were viable at time of publication. Another use of technology can be made with webquests such as the one featured in the theme "Traverse the Universe." More detailed information on how to find, create, and make use of webquests is included in this theme.

Employing one or two commercially prepared items that might go with your theme and center units is a way to save time and stress, especially if staff is at a minimum. After completing the theme "Summer Down Under" I came across a jigsaw-puzzle book called *Australian Animals Jigsaw Book* by Garry Fleming. A quick search on the Internet led me to Five Mile Press, an Australian publisher (http://www.fivemile.com.au), and I decided this might compliment the subtheme "Walkabout the Outback."

The "Add Pizzazz" section is included at the end of unit plans in each fully developed theme to embellish the fun and intrigue of your exhibit and centers-based SRP. Hiring storytellers or performers with related repertoires, holding specially planned events, or simply adding background music or authentic-looking artifacts as an extra display may require more work and funding, but are suggestions for further inspiration. Use your imagination to develop these extra frills as your grant seeking, budget, time, and staff permit.

Finally, promoting your collection with a list of theme-related books for each unit, culminating with a bibliography and summer-long display of good related fiction, rounds out your program and makes your collection more attractive and inviting.

Following this chapter are complete, detailed outlines and content for three themes designed around an interactive-centers approach. These three themes, "Summer Down Under: An

Use Computers and the Web to

Enhance exhibit concepts with
Visual and Auditory exposure

Awesome Aussie Experience," "The Invention Convention," and "Traverse the Universe" all include models for incorporating art, writing, reading, technology, science, mathematics and, of course, children's literature. These sample themes also include a game-sheet much like a bingo board that can be designed with small incremental goals and completion certificates for those who wish to keep some of the traditional incentive opportunities intact. These complete themed programs will serve as models for you to develop other summer reading themes. Following these three complete plans are five more outlines with initial resources for additional theme subtopics that you may develop into content-rich interactive centers using the above examples and guidelines.

How you choose to create your centers will depend on the expectations and goals you set out for your community and library programs. The combination of your ingenuity, creativity, staff, volunteers, children, and families will fuse together for successful, interactive exhibits and centers-based summer reading programs.

7

Summer Down Under: An Awesome Aussie Experience

Outline of Program

Weeks 1 & 2—The Lucky Country, Australia
1. Get to know the country known as Oz (national symbols, etc.)
2. Australia's slang language
3. Geography
4. Cuisine
5. Geology and climate

Weeks 3 & 4—Walkabout the Outback
1. Wildlife and plants
2. Great Barrier Reef
3. Aboriginal people/society

Weeks 5 & 6—Dreamtime: The Aboriginal Arts
1. Music
2. Art
3. Storytelling

Weeks 7 & 8—Back in Time with Australia's Fascinating History
1. Historical timeline
2. Exploration of Australia
3. Penal colony and Britain
4. Noteworthy Australians

Australia's unique natural and man-made wonders can provide enormous possibilities for a summer-long exhibition. From its animals to its Great Barrier Reef, from its distinctive history and Aboriginal population to its exploration and colonization, from its undeveloped landscape to its beautifully modern developed cities, multiple interactive centers offer learning, discovery, and fun with four units grouped as follows.

Summer Down Under G'Day Game Sheet

Ask a librarian to stamp your game sheet with a 'Roo for every box you complete.

Attend a Program	Read for One Hour	Read an "Illywhacker" (Tall Tale)	Read for One Hour	Attend a Program
Read for 1/2 Hour	Poetry Potpourri (Read a Book of Poems)	Finish an Aussie Interactive Center	Find the Dewey Number for Books on Australia	Read for 1/2 Hour
Read for One Hour	Find the Dewey Number for Koalas & Kangaroos	Attend the Open House Kickoff	Read a Fairytale or a Picture Book	Read for One Hour
Read for 1/2 Hour	Finish an Aussie Interactive Center	Read a Short Story	Finish an Aussie Interactive Center	Read for 1/2 Hour
Attend a Program	Read for One Hour	Finish an Aussie Interactive Center	Read for One Hour	Attend a Program

5 Boxes Stamped = Your Name on the Koala Tree

10 Boxes Stamped = Your Name on the 'Roo Board

15 Boxes Stamped = Your Name on a Bonzer Certificate

Summer Down Under
Summer Reading Program

▶ Register.

▶ Read-to-Me to Grade 8 may participate.

▶ Take your reading game sheet home and
  READ, READ, READ!
  Keep track of the time you spend reading.

▶ Participate in our interactive centers and attend
  library programs!

▶ When you've completed a box on your game sheet,
  ask a librarian to stamp the appropriate box.

▶ Complete 5 boxes — put your name
  on the Koala tree.

▶ Complete 10 boxes — put your name
  on the Kangaroo Board.

▶ Complete 15 boxes — receive a Bonzer Certificate,
  a Boomerang, Books, or a coupon.

▶ Complete all boxes — receive an entry
  in the Grand Prize Drawing!

▶ The LAST DAY to have game sheets stamped
  is _____.

▶ Enter the weekly lotto each time you visit the
  library (one entry per day) for a chance to win
  a _____. You must be registered in
  Summer Reading to enter.

From *Summer Reading Renaissance: An Interactive Exhibits Approach* by Rita Soltan. Illustrations by Jill Reichenbach Fill. Westport, CT: Libraries Unlimited. Copyright © 2008.

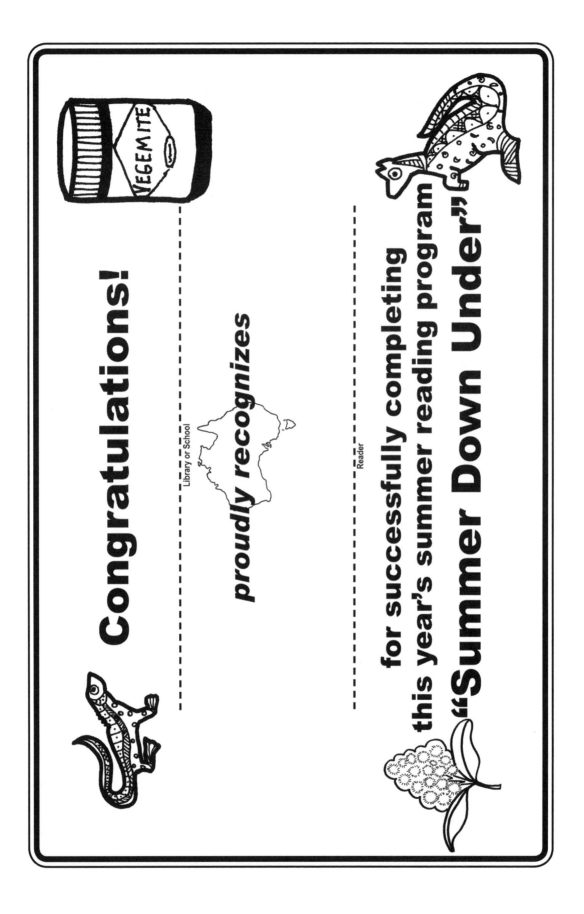

Congratulations!

_____
Library or School

proudly recognizes

_____
Reader

for successfully completing
this year's summer reading program
"Summer Down Under"

Unit 1 The Lucky Country, Australia

Establish the theme or topic with this unit to introduce the continent and country through an overview of interesting facts and Australian specifics. Participants can discover why Australia is known as "The Lucky Country" or "OZ," that its slang language is referred to as "strine," its location is below the equator and how this affects its climate and weather, favorite "tucker" or food, some basic geography, and even some geological tidbits.

Resources for This Unit

Arnold, Caroline. 2003. *Ulluru: Australia's Aboriginal Heart.* Photographs by Arthur Arnold. New York: Clarion Books.

Five Mile Press. 1996. *My First Atlas of Australia.* Noble Park Victoria: Five Mile Press.

Germaine, Elizabeth, and Ann L. Burckhardt. 1990. *Cooking the Australian Way.* Photographs by Robert L. and Diane Wolfe. Minneapolis: Lerner.

Heiman, Sarah. 2003. *Australia ABCs.* Illustrated by Arturo Avila. Minneapolis: Picture Window Books.

Heinrichs, Ann. 1998. *Australia.* New York: Children's Press.

Olawsky, Lynn Ainsworth. 1997. *Colors of Australia.* Illustrations by Janice Lee Porter. Minneapolis: Carolrhoda.

Rose, Elizabeth. 2004. *A Primary Source Guide to Australia.* New York: Rosen.

Somervill, Barbara. 2004. *Geography of the World: Australia.* Chanhassen, MN: The Child's World.

Web Sites

Australian Government: It's An Honour Australia Celebrating Australia. http://www.itsanhonour.gov.au/.

Australia Day. http://www.australiaday.com.au/.

Keep a stack of the following fact sheet available together with a mounted copy on display by your exhibit area.

Facts About Australia, the Lucky Country

- Australia is the only country in the world that is also a continent.
- Australia is the sixth largest country in the world.
- Australia is made up of six states and two territories.

  - New South Wales
  - Queensland
  - Victoria
  - South Australia
  - Western Australia
  - Tasmania
  - Canberra, the Capital Territory
  - Northern Territory

- About 20 million people live in Australia, 70% in the 10 largest cities.

  - Australia is one of the driest continents in the world.

- Australia has

  - rainforests and vast plains in the north
  - snowfields in the southeast
  - desert in the center
  - fertile croplands in the east, south, and southwest

- The official language of Australia is English.

  - Its slang is known as "strine."

- Australia's major industries are mining and farming.
- Australia's government is headed by a Prime Minister, but is also under the British Monarch.

For more interesting facts log onto http://www.australia.gov.au/about-australia.

From *Summer Reading Renaissance: An Interactive Exhibits Approach* by Rita Soltan. Illustrations by Jill Reichenbach Fill. Westport, CT: Libraries Unlimited. Copyright © 2008.

INTERACTIVE CENTER 1

CREATE A BANNER

Materials Needed

Poster paper
Markers or poster paint
Construction paper
Scissors
Glue sticks
Mini stars

Banner

Use the outline below as a guide for the banner. The banner can be used as an overall display to introduce your SRP theme.

"The Lucky Country: OZ"

Flags—National and Aboriginal
National colors—green and gold
National flower—the golden wattle
Native animals—kangaroo and emu
National gemstone—the opal
National holiday—January 26, Australia Day

How Participants Can Interact

Children can create their own bumper sticker from the banner model and flags
from the samples below.

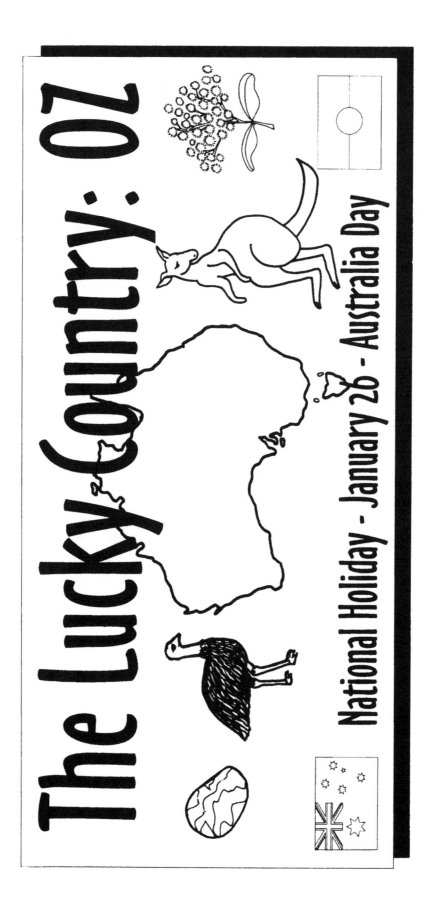

The Lucky Country: OZ 70

National Holiday – January 26 – Australia Day

National Flag of Australia

Red → small diagonal lines

Red

Blue

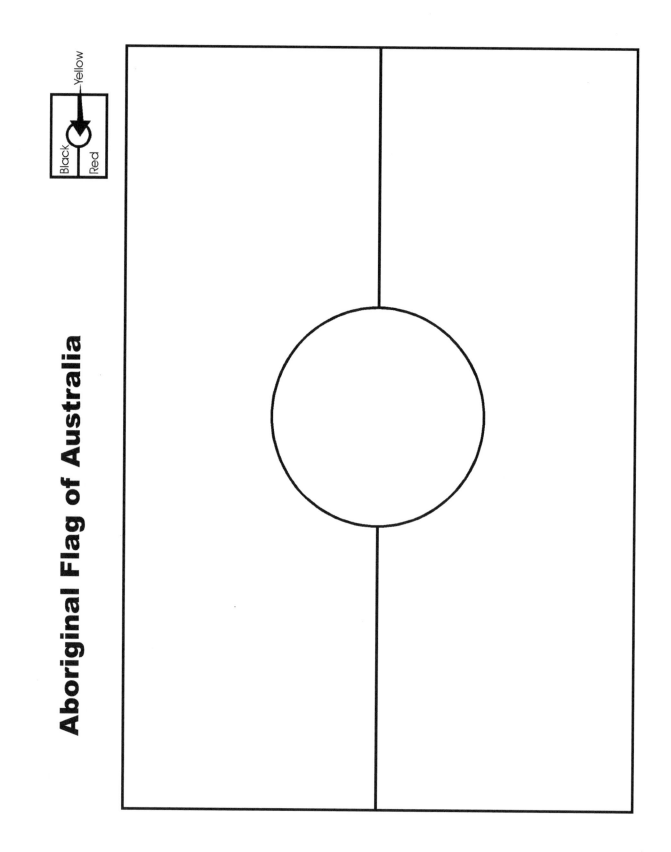

Aboriginal Flag of Australia

Black · Yellow · Red

INTERACTIVE CENTER 2

GEOGRAPHY OF AUSTRALIA

Materials Needed

Blank map of Australia
Blank map of the United States
Variety of maps of Australia and the United States through books and atlas resources, or even a current globe
Pencils, crayons

How Participants Can Interact

Participants can recreate two maps using the resources provided and compare and contrast size and shape of the map of Australia with the map of the United States.

Directions for Participants

- Australia is about the same size as the mainland of the United States. Use the two maps to compare and contrast the size and shape of the two large countries.
- How many places can you fill in on the Australian map? Use the resources at the table to help you.

  - Western Australia
  - Northern Territory
  - Queensland
  - New South Wales
  - Sydney
  - Canberra
  - South Australia
  - Tasmania
  - Indian Ocean
  - Pacific Ocean
  - Great Barrier Reef
  - Perth
  - Victoria
  - Adelaide
  - Melbourne
  - Brisbane
  - Coral Sea

- Fill in the states on the U.S. map.
- Color your two maps when you are finished.
- Cut around the outline of both maps.
- Place the U.S. map over the map of Australia and see how their sizes compare.

Australia

From *Summer Reading Renaissance: An Interactive Exhibits Approach* by Rita Soltan. Illustrations by Jill Reichenbach Fill. Westport, CT: Libraries Unlimited. Copyright © 2008.

80

The United States

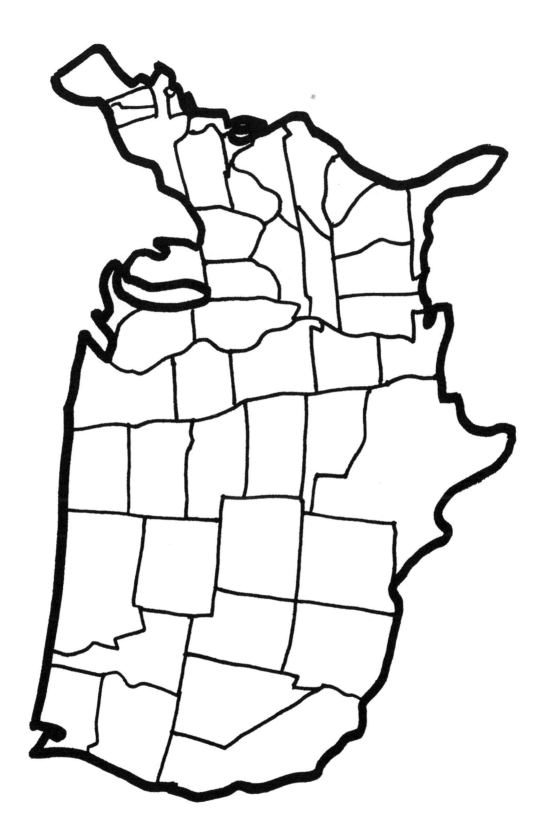

From *Summer Reading Renaissance: An Interactive Exhibits Approach* by Rita Soltan. Illustrations by Jill Reichenbach Fill. Westport, CT: Libraries Unlimited. Copyright © 2008.

INTERACTIVE CENTER 3

STRINE LANGUAGE OF AUSTRALIA

While the official language of Australia is English, brought over by the British, a dialect or slang language called "strine" (short for Au-strine and a shortened pronunciation of Australian) has evolved over the years and is very popular.

Print up a version of the glossary below.

Materials Needed

Printed copies of glossary of strine (below)
Printed copies of crossword puzzle (below)
A word game set like Scrabble
Internet station
Pencils

How Participants Can Interact

Have children work on the Strine Crossword Puzzle below or bring in a word game set and have participants play using only strine language.

Numerous other word games can be created, such as Hangman. For an online version check out *Billabong Words* (http://www.fraynework.com.au/story/words/index.html) and have it bookmarked on one of your Internet stations.

You may also refer to the Aussie Slang Dictionary (http://www.koalanet.com.au/australian-slang.html) for more Aussie words and expressions

Words and Expressions to
Help You Sound Like a Real Aussie

Ace!	excellent! very good!
Apples, she'll be	it'll be all right
Arvo	afternoon
Ankle biter	small child
Barbie	barbecue
Bathers	swimming suit
Bikkie	biscuit
It cost big bikkies	it was expensive
Billy	teapot
Bloke	man
Bonzer	great
Bush	the hinterland, the outback, not in town
Bushie	someone who lives in the Bush
Bush telly	campfire
Cactus	dead, not functioning (this car is cactus)
Chemist's	drugstore
Chook	chicken
Chewie	chewing gum
Chokkie	chocolate
Cobber	friend
Corroboree	an Aboriginal festival or get together
Daks	trousers
Down Under	Australia and New Zealand
Drum	information
I'll give you the drum	I'll give you the information or low-down
Fair dinkum	really, honestly
G'day	hello
Good onya	good for you, well done!
Hooroo	good-bye
Jackaroo	boy rancher
Jillaroo	girl rancher
Joey	baby
Jumbuck	sheep
Jumper	sweater
Jug	electric kettle
Lollies	candy
London to a brick	it's absolutely certain
Mate	buddy, friend
Never Never	the very remote Outback
Oz	Australia
Prezzy	a present, gift
Rage	party
Roo	Kangaroo
Sanger	sandwich
Station	a big farm
Stoked	very pleased
Sunnies	sunglasses
Tucker	food
Unit	apartment/flat
Walkabout	a long walk or rambling trip
Water biscuit	cracker

STRINE CROSSWORD

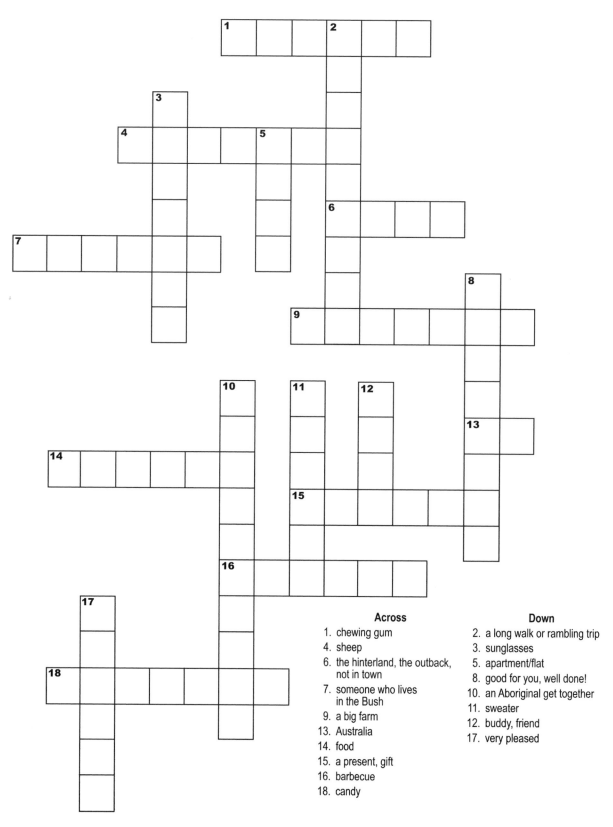

Across

1. chewing gum
4. sheep
6. the hinterland, the outback, not in town
7. someone who lives in the Bush
9. a big farm
13. Australia
14. food
15. a present, gift
16. barbecue
18. candy

Down

2. a long walk or rambling trip
3. sunglasses
5. apartment/flat
8. good for you, well done!
10. an Aboriginal get together
11. sweater
12. buddy, friend
17. very pleased

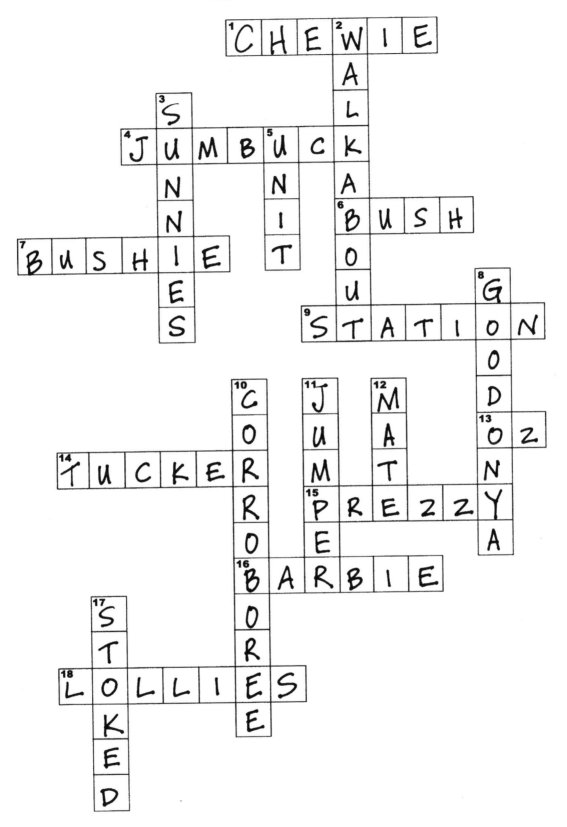

INTERACTIVE CENTER 4

AUSTRALIAN CUISINE: DISCOVER THE VARIOUS FOODS OF AUSTRALIA
Materials Needed

Copies of *Possum Magic* by Mem Fox
Large map of Australia indicating major cities—laminated, if possible
Stack of copies of blank map of Australia for each participant

How Participants Can Interact

1. Children and parents can read Fox's story together and to one another and recreate the map on the last page. Encourage participants to pay attention and reflect on the last page indicating cities and food explanations mentioned in the story.

Directions for Participants

- Read *Possum Magic* alone, with a parent, or with a friend.
- Look at the last page where all the cities mentioned in the story are located on a map of Australia.
- Take a blank map and mark all the cities Hush and Grandma Poss visited.
- Draw a picture of each kind of food Hush and Grandma Poss ate next to the city on your map.
- Mark the path the characters took along the way through the Australian cities.
- Color your map.

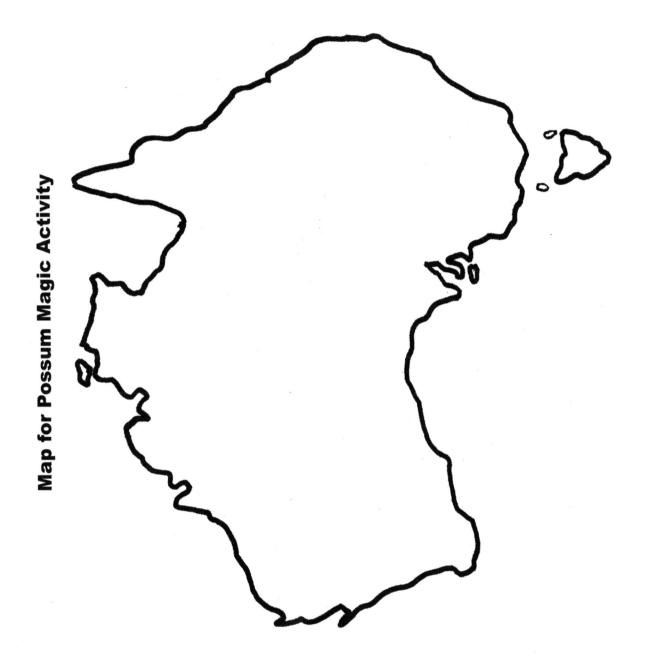

2.   Children may also create a recipe book for an Aussie Arvo Tea. A nice follow-up to the recipe book might be to offer a tasting station with samples of each food.

Tea is an afternoon (arvo) staple in Australia. Menus may consist of small sandwiches and pastries along with a pot of tea. Children may substitute herbal fruit-flavored tea.

Materials Needed

Copies of four recipes printed on 8 1/2 × 5 1/2 paper (normal copy paper cut in half)
Sheets of 8 1/2 x 5 1/2 multicolored construction paper
Wrapping ribbon or yarn strips cut into 24-inch strips
Individual hole punch
Crayons or markers

Making Your Arvo Tea Recipe Book

Gather all four recipe sheets plus two cover sheets and organize them into a book.
Punch two holes on the left side of your book.
Tie your book together with a ribbon or piece of yarn.
Decorate the cover of your recipe book, then take it home and cook away!
Find these and other Australian recipes at:
    http://www.recipesource.com/ethnic/asia/australian/.

Cucumber Mini Sandwiches

6 slices of white bread with crusts removed

1 large seedless cucumber

Margarine or butter spread

Coat the bread slices with the margarine or butter spread. Cut the cucumber into thin 1/8-inch round slices. Layer a few cucumber slices on three bread slices and cover each with the remaining three bread slices. Cut the three sandwiches into quarter triangles.

Serves 4-6.

Mem Fox includes a Vegemite Sandwich as one of the foods in her story.

Vegemite spread thinly on toast is a popular snack. Vegemite is a pasty mixture made from vegetable extract and brewer's yeast. It is a great source for vitamin B and often is an Australian baby's first solid food. Check out the website http://www.vegemite.com.au/ for both current and historical information on this Australian favorite staple. For Americans, this spread can be quite strong and sometimes repellant in flavor.

Anzac Biscuits (Cookies)

Australia commemorates its fallen soldiers every April 25 on Anzac Day, named after the Australian and New Zealand Army Corps that suffered its worst defeat during World War I.

3/4 cup sugar

1 tsp. honey or corn syrup

1/4 lb. butter

1 tsp. baking soda

3/4 cup shredded coconut

1 cup oats

3/4 cup flour

2 tbsp. boiling water

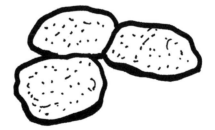

In a saucepan place butter, honey or corn syrup, baking soda, sugar and mix with boiling water. Bring slowly to boil, remove and add oats, coconut, flour, sugar. Mix well. Place spoonfuls about 3 inches apart on a cookie tray lined with parchment paper. Bake at 275° F about 25 minutes or until crisp and golden. Cool on a wire rack before removing with a spatula. Makes about 30 cookies.

Pavlova

This is a favorite dessert made of meringue topped off with whipped cream and sliced fresh strawberries and kiwi. The trick to making a good meringue is to start off with a very clean, dry mixing bowl. Australians make one very large meringue that they then cover with whipped cream and fruit. However, this recipe will also make 20 individual small meringues, which will take a shorter time to cook and be easier to serve.

4 egg whites

1 cup sugar

1/2 tsp. vanilla

1/2 pint heavy whipping cream or ready-made whipped cream

Sliced fresh strawberries and kiwi fruit

Let the egg whites stand at room temperature for at least 20 minutes. Beat rapidly until they stiffen and form peaks. Add the sugar and continue beating. Fold in the vanilla. Drop small circles of the beaten egg whites onto a cookie sheet lined with parchment paper. Bake 20 minutes at 275° F. They should be firm to touch. Remove and let cool. Whip the heavy cream until stiff. Spread some whipped cream onto each meringue and top with a slice of strawberry and kiwi fruit.

Lamington

These are little sponge cakes dipped in chocolate sauce and topped with coconut shreds.

1 commercial yellow cake mix

1 lb. can of your favorite chocolate syrup

1 package of shredded coconut

Make the yellow cake mix according to box directions in a square baking dish. Once cake is baked and cooled, cut into even squares. Pour the chocolate syrup into a bowl. Open the coconut into another bowl. Using tongs, dip each cake square into the chocolate syrup until covered and then into the bowl of shredded coconut. Place each square onto a serving plate and wait until they harden a bit.

Makes 10-12 lamingtons.

From *Summer Reading Renaissance: An Interactive Exhibits Approach* by Rita Soltan. Illustrations by Jill Reichenbach Fill. Westport, CT: Libraries Unlimited. Copyright © 2008.

INTERACTIVE CENTER 5

GEOLOGICAL WONDERS AND THE CLIMATE DOWN UNDER

In the center of Australia is a natural geological phenomenon in the form of a huge sandstone rock that rises from the desert floor and reaches more than 1,000 feet high. It is the world's largest rock. For many years it was known as Ayers Rock. The Aborigines or native people have always called this giant red rock Uluru and consider it a sacred site, connected to their spiritual and religious beliefs about the creation of the land and all its creatures.

Download a picture of Uluru from http://en.wikipedia.org/wiki/Image:Uluru2.jpg.

How Participants Can Interact

Set up an online tour of Uluru at an Internet station with one of these Web sites:

Australian Explorer: Uluru, Ayers Rock
    http://www.australianexplorer.com/uluru.htm

or

Australian Government Department of the Environment, Water, Heritage and
    the Arts
Uluru—Kata Tjuta National Park
    http://www.deh.gov.au/parks/uluru/index.html.

Australia's Climate

Australia's position on the globe is below the equator. The northern part of the country (40%) falls within the tropics, resulting in two seasons that are wet (November to April) and dry (May to October). In addition, the Tropic of Capricorn runs across Australia. The southern part of the country experiences four seasons:

Summer—December to February
Autumn—March to May
Winter—June to August
Spring—September to November

How Participants Can Interact

Create a weather wheel to illustrate Australia's seasons opposite those in northern hemisphere countries such as the United States.

Materials Needed

Globe or map of the world indicating Australia's position below the equator and
    United States above the equator
White card stock 8 1/2 x 11 inches
Protractor and/or circle template

Weather Wheel.

Ruler
Pencils, crayons, markers
Paper fasteners
Scissors

Post a list of directions from the outline below. Parents or adults may help children read and follow accordingly.

Directions for Making a Weather Wheel

- Take two pieces of card stock.
- Use the protractor or circle template to create a large circle (with a diameter that stretches from one side to the other) on one piece of card stock.
- Cut out the circle.
- Make a smaller circle (diameter about 2 inches smaller) on the second piece of card stock.
- Cut out the second circle.
- Using the ruler, divide both circles into four equal parts.

- Write the four seasons—summer, fall, winter, spring—on each quarterfor both circles.
- On the larger circle write the months for the seasons for the United States.
- On the smaller circle, write the months for the seasons for Australia.
- Use this chart to help you:

U.S. Seasons

Summer—June to August
Autumn—September to November
Winter—December to February
Spring—March to May

Australia's Seasons

Summer—December to February
Autumn—March to May
Winter—June to August
Spring—September to November

- Place the two circles together with the months of the year matching each quarter.
- Use a paper fastener to make a hole through the two circles or ask an adult to help you.
- Fasten the circles together.
- Decorate your weather wheel with seasonal symbols and use it to tell you how the seasons in the two countries are opposite each other.

Unit 2 Walkabout the Outback

Australia's Bush and Great Barrier Reef are filled with animals and plants unique to its separate continent and environment. Familiar kangaroos, unfriendly Tasmanian devils, and other marsupials, birds, and unique egg-laying mammals such as the platypus and echidna can intrigue youngsters and parents alike. The Aboriginal civilization can also be introduced here as both past and present inhabitants.

Resources for This Unit

Banting, Erinn. 2005. *Natural Wonders: The Great Barrier Reef, The Largest Coral Reef in the World.* New York: Weigl Publishers.

Bartlett, Anne. 2002. *The Aboriginal Peoples of Australia.* Minneapolis: Lerner.

Bauman, Amy. 2000. *Kangaroos.* Photographs by Steve Parish. Milwaukee, WI: Gareth Stevens.

Grupper, Jonathan. 2000. *Destination: Australia.* Washington, DC: National Geographic Society.

McGovern, Ann. 1989. *Down Under Down Under: Diving Adventures on the Great Barrier Reef.* Photographs by Jim and Martin Scheiner, and the author. New York: Macmillan.

Parish, Steve. 2003. *Australian Wildlife.* Broomall, PA: Mason Crest.

Sharp, Anne Wallace. 2003. *Indigenous Peoples of the World: Australia.* San Diego: Lucent Books.

Sotzek, Hannelore, and Bobbie Kalman. 1997. *A Koala is Not a Bear!* New York: Crabtree.

Vaughan, Marcia K. 1986. *Wombat Stew.* Illustrated by Pamela Lofts. Morristown, NJ: Silver Burdett.

Votaw, Carol. 2007. *Waking Up Down Under.* Illustrated by Susan Banta. Minnetonka, MN: NorthWord.

INTERACTIVE CENTER 1

AUSTRALIA'S WILDLIFE AND PLANTS

Australia's continent was formed, 65 million years ago, when the supercontinent of Pangaea divided. Australia drifted farther away from all the other continents. For a good explanation on this theory log on to http://volcano.und.edu/vwdocs/vwlessons/lessons/Pangea/Pangea1.html.

Australia's independent position away from the rest of the continents allowed it to develop some unique and strange animals and plants that are native only to its land and environment.

How Participants Can Interact

Create an information center with a display board offering pictures and brief notes for each of the following Australian animals:

Kangaroo, Tasmanian Devil, Sugar Glider, Platypus, Emu, Echidna, Koala, Kookaburra, Wombat

Your center may include an Internet station that can allow visual exploration of these animals through two Web sites for Australia's plant and wildlife.

The Perth Zoo:
  http://www.perthzoo.wa.gov.au/Animals—Plants/.
Australia's National Zoo and Aquarium:
  http://www.zooquarium.com.au/index.htm.

With both sites, children and parents may explore, view, and read about the animals mentioned above and others not normally seen in our part of the world. The Perth Zoo site offers an A-Z online tour of both animals and plants that is well worth taking.

How Participants Can Interact

Have the book *Wombat Stew* by Marcia Vaughan, illustrated by Pamela Lofts, available at the center (see resource list above). Younger children can create stick puppets for their favorite Australian animal from the patterns below after reading the book alone, or with a parent or friend.

Make templates for the animals from the patterns provided.

Materials Needed

White paper plates
Markers, crayons, pencils

Scissors
Large craft sticks
Glue or glue sticks

Directions for Participants

- Take one of the animal templates and trace it on a paper plate.
- Cut out your animal.
- Color it. You may use books or the display to help you.
- Take a craft stick and glue it behind your animal to finish your stick puppet.
- Tell the story again with your stick puppets.

INTERACTIVE CENTER 2
THE GREAT BARRIER REEF

Considered one of the Seven Wonders of the Natural World, Australia hosts the largest coral reef, an important ecosystem where animals and plants interrelate within their underwater environment.

How Participants Can Interact

Set up an Internet station with this National Geographic site:
   http://www.nationalgeographic.com/earthpulse/reef/reef1_flash.html.
Participants can be introduced to this "underwater Eden" and learn about the unique flora and fauna as they "dive into" the tour provided.
You may also refer to the Australian Government Great Barrier Reef Marine Park Authority Web site below for more information to help you establish your information center:
   http://www.gbrmpa.gov.au/.
Other books on coral reefs:

   Brinkworth, Brian. 2006. *Life in a Coral Reef.* New York: Rosen.
   Collard, Sneed B. 2006. *On the Coral Reefs.* New York: Marshall Cavendish.
   Furgang, Kathy. 2000. *Let's Take a Field Trip to a Coral Reef.* New York: Rosen.

How Participants Can Interact

After reading about the coral reef, participants can create some origami animals.
Two illustrated books can be left at this center for older and younger children to read and explore.
In *Old Shell, New Shell* by Helen Ward (Brookfield, CT: Millbrook, 2002), a hermit crab moves through the coral reef looking for a new shell.
One Night in the Coral Sea by Sneed B. Collard III (Watertown, MA: Charlesbridge, 2004) beautifully explains. along with Robin Brickman's paintings, the annual mass-spawning event of the corals that occurs on only one day.
Read and explore the information in either book with a parent or friend.

Materials Needed

Origami Paper
Copies of the book *Underwater Origami: Aquatic Paper Folding for Kids* by Steve and Megumi Biddle (Hauppauge, NY: Barron's Educational Series, 2000).

This book is a treasure trove of underwater origami creations. In particular, you may refer to instructions for making Coral (p. 5), a Conch Shell (p. 6), a Starfish (p. 8), a Crab (p. 13), and a Sea Horse (p. 22), all creatures of the Barrier Reef.

Be sure to make these ahead to display as examples together with printed copies of instructions providing proper credit to the publication.

INTERACTIVE CENTER 3

Who Are the Aboriginal People?

Like the European explorers who encountered the Native American Indians on North America's lands, British and other European settlers in the 1700s were greeted by Australia's native inhabitants, dubbed "Aborigines" from the Latin word meaning "from the beginning." The Aborigines encompassed numerous groups around the mainland, the southern island of Tasmania, and the Torres Strait Islands in the north.

How Participants Can Interact

Create an original board game using the templates. Copy the true/false statements for information about the Aboriginal people onto index cards cut in half. You should have a total of 35–40 statements. You may make up more true or false statements using the recommended resources as well.

Name of Game: Aborigine Actuality

Materials Needed

Tag board
Large die
Word processor
Copy machine
Small index cards
Pens or markers

Facts for Aborigine Actuality

TRUE STATEMENTS (Make a card for each true statement with the word *True* on the reverse)

1. The word aborigine comes from the Latin meaning "from the beginning."
2. The native inhabitants of Australia were named "Aborigines" by the European explorers.
3. Aboriginal people believe their ancestors were created at the beginning of the world.
4. Aboriginal people are considered to be the oldest living culture in the world.
5. Aborigines led a nomadic life moving around the continent as the climate changed.
6. Aborigines lived in clans or tribes.
7. Each clan had its own language and rituals.
8. Aborigines have a rich culture and spiritual heritage.
9. The Aboriginal population numbered more than one million prior to European settlement.
10. The arrival of the Europeans brought disease, devastation, and change to the life of the Aborigines.
11. The plight of Native American Indian society is similar to that of the Australian Aborigine.
12. The Aborigines lived off the land, hunting and fishing.
13. The boomerang was invented as a hunting weapon.
14. Some tribes ate marsupials and kangaroos.
15. Plants formed the mainstay of the Aboriginal diet with wild tomatoes called *wamulu*, bush raisins, and wild onions.
16. The Aborigines spiritual life centers around their belief in the Dreamtime—the creation of the world.
17. The land is sacred for the Aborigines as it holds the spirits of their ancestors.
18. Storytelling is an important part of everyday life for the Aborigine. It is used to pass on the knowledge of their heritage.
19. Rock Art is a way of recording the Aborigine history.
20. Aborigines love music and use song and a variety of instruments like the didgeridoo.

FALSE STATEMENTS (*Includes the correct statement, which you may write on the reverse of each false card*)

1. The Aboriginal Flag is the same as the Australian National Flag. (*They have their own flag.*)
2. All Aboriginal people are dark skinned. (*Many modern Aborigines have European blood and may have fair skin and hair.*)
3. All Aboriginal people live in the Outback. (*Many live in the large cities today.*)
4. The different tribes of the Aboriginal people have different religions. (*They have different languages and rituals but share a common religion.*)
5. The Aborigines always lived in Australia from the beginning of time. (*Scientists believe their ancestors came from parts of Asia or Africa and may have walked across the bridges of land that used to connect the continents.*)

6. In traditional Aboriginal culture, the individual is most important. *(Community and family are most important.)*
7. The arts are something Aborigines do not like to participate in. *(Everyone is considered an artist through their everyday life of painting, music, and storytelling.)*
8. The main musical instrument for the Aboriginal people is the didgeridoo. *(Singing with the human voice is considered the first instrument.)*
9. Corroboree is a rare plant in the Outback. *(It is the traditional festival Aborigines hold to honor the spirits.)*
10. Aborigines used fire just for cooking. *(Fire-stick farming, by regularly burning off bushes and undergrowth, maintained the grasslands.)*
11. Aborigines were and are a violent people. *(They lived peacefully together for 40,000 years, sharing everything between tribes as is their belief and custom.)*
12. The European settlers got along well with the Aboriginal people. *(There was a culture clash and they did not understand each other's practices and way of life.)*
13. The Aborigines were able to resist the smallpox, measles, and influenza brought with the European explorers. *(Thousands died because they had never been exposed to such disease.)*
14. The Church and the missionaries (teachers of Christianity) were welcomed by the Aboriginal people. *(Many were forced to give up their Aboriginal culture and attend church-run schools and live in church-run homes.)*
15. The Aborigines were always treated equally to the Australian white population. *(Only recently, since the 1967 Referendum, have Aborigines begun to be included as part of Australian society. The Australian Council for Aboriginal Reconciliation was established in 1991.)*

From *Summer Reading Renaissance: An Interactive Exhibits Approach* by Rita Soltan. Illustrations by Jill Reichenbach Fill. Westport, CT: Libraries Unlimited. Copyright © 2008.

Game Directions

- Choose a token.
- Each player rolls the die. Player with highest number goes first.
- Player rolls die to determine number of moves.
- Player chooses a question card and must answer it correctly to move.
- First player to move to end of board is winner.

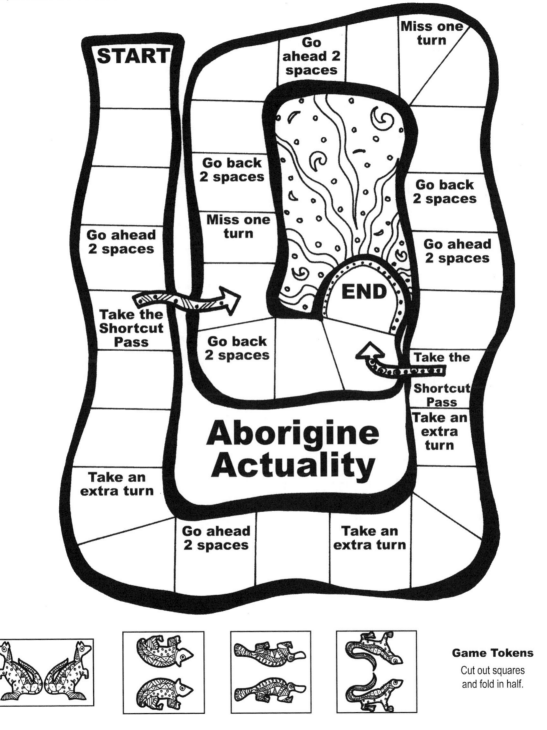

START

Go ahead 2 spaces

Miss one turn

Go back 2 spaces

Miss one turn

Go back 2 spaces

Go ahead 2 spaces

END

Go ahead 2 spaces

Take the Shortcut Pass

Go back 2 spaces

Take the Shortcut Pass

Take an extra turn

Aborigine Actuality

Take an extra turn

Go ahead 2 spaces

Take an extra turn

Game Tokens
Cut out squares
and fold in half.

INTERACTIVE CENTER 4

VISITING THE ARNHEM LAND

In the picture book *Ernie Dances to the Didgeridoo* by Alison Lester (Boston: Houghton Mifflin, 2001), younger children may be introduced to life in an Aboriginal community called Gunbalanya. Ernie moves from the city to the Arnhem Land in northern Australia when his parents begin work in a hospital. There he learns about life, customs, the seasons, and the language of the Aborigines.

How Participants Can Interact

Reading the book can provide opportunity for discussion and some critical thinking about life in an Australian Outback community. A question board displayed near the book can spark ideas for participants to consider and talk about.

Arnhem Land Activity Turtle's Shell
Materials Needed

Arnhem Land turtle template
Markers, pencils, crayons, scissors
Read Ernie's story, *Ernie Dances to the Didgeridoo,* alone or with a parent or friend.
Use these questions to help you talk about Ernie's experience with the Gunbalanya
people.

- How is life different for the Gunbalanya children Ernie meets in Arnhem Land?
- What kinds of animals does Ernie find and learn about?
- What is the weather like in Arnhem Land? How does it change for each season?
- What does Ernie like to do?

After talking about the book, fill in the turtle's shell with Arnhem Land activities using pictures or words. Fill in the turtle's face and feet. Cut out your Arnhem Land activity turtle.

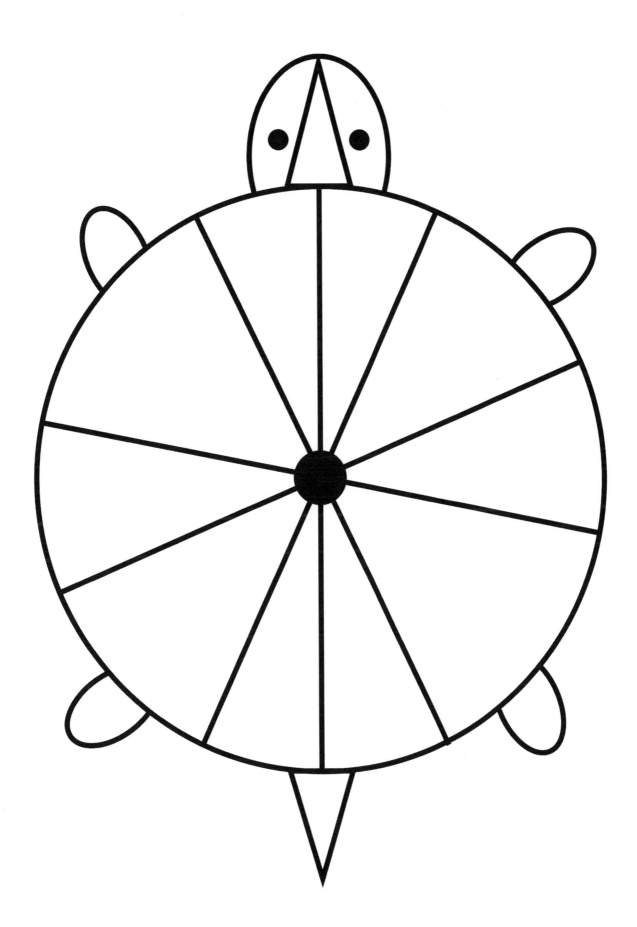

Unit 3 Dreamtime: the Aboriginal Arts and Music

Central to the Aboriginal life is the belief in the spiritual concept called Dreamtime. Dreamtime is related to the creation of the world by the Ancestors who left behind a legacy of rules and laws to live by. The Aborigines believe the spirits of these Ancestors lie in the earth, its mountains, rivers, and rocks—everywhere in the land. Much of the arts are connected to this ancient religion.

In this unit, families can experiment with musical instruments like didgeridoos and clap sticks, storytelling through rock painting, and the folklore of this indigenous society.

Resources for This Unit

Bartlett, Anne. 2002. *The Aboriginal Peoples of Australia.* Minneapolis: Lerner.
Czernecki, Stefan, and Timothy Rhodes. 1993. *The Singing Snake.* New York: Hyperion.
Finley, Carol. 1999. *Aboriginal Art of Australia: Exploring Cultural Traditions.* Minneapolis: Lerner.
Germein, Katrina. 1999. *Big Rain Coming.* Illustrated by Bronwyn Bancroft. New York: Clarion Books.
Maddern, Eric. 1993. *The Rainbow Bird: An Aboriginal Folktale from Northern Australia.* Illustrated by Adrienne Kennaway. Boston: Little, Brown, and Company.
McKay, Helen F., ed. 2001. *Gadi Mirabooka: Australian Aboriginal Tales from the Dreaming.* Westport, CT: Libraries Unlimited.
Morgan, Sally. 1992. *The Flying Emu and Other Australian Stories.* New York: Alfred A. Knopf.
Oodgeroo. 1994. *Dreamtime: Aboriginal Stories.* Illustrated by Bronwyn Bancroft. New York: Lothrop, Lee, Shepard.
Roth, Susan L. 1996. *The Biggest Frog in Australia.* New York: Simon & Schuster.
Wolkstein, Diane. 2004. *Sun Mother Wakes the World: An Australian Creation Story.* Pictures by Bronwyn Bancroft. New York: HarperCollins.

Web Sites

Answers to common questions asked by kids about the Aboriginal people:
Indigenous Australia—How Do I Find . . . ?
http://www.dreamtime.net.au/kids/how.cfm.
Indigenous Australia—for Teachers:
http://www.dreamtime.net.au/teachers/index.cfm.
Stories to watch and listen to on the web:
Indigenous Australia—Stories
http://www.dreamtime.net.au/dreaming/storylist.htm.

INTERACTIVE CENTER 1

MUSICAL INSTRUMENTS OF THE ABORIGINES

Music plays a large role in the cultural life of the Aboriginal people. In addition to songs associated with the Dreamtime, music is part of the traditional Corroboree, the Aborigine celebration and festival. The Didgeridoo is one of the most well-known instruments.

A wealth of information on the Aboriginal music culture can be obtained at the following Web site: http://www.aboriginalart.com.au/didgeridoo/.

In addition, the following 24-minute video recording can be used as a visual portion of your display:

David Hudson. 1999. *David Hudson: Making and Playing Didgeridoo.* Balmain, NSW: Oceanic Music.

The song "What is a Didjeridoo?" is featured on the CD by Tom Chapin on his 1996 album, *Around the World and Back Again.* New York: Sony Music Entertainment Inc.

How Participants Can Interact

Create an information center about the didgeridoo and clap sticks. Display some of the books listed in the resources above as an example of the artwork that may be created.

- The word didgeridoo means "drone pipe."
- A didgeridoo is made from a single long hollow bamboo branch or other tree branch.
- The sound created by a didgeridoo sometimes sounds like a foghorn. Other times it can produce a high squeal or a low droning noise.
- The didgeridoo is decorated with painting that reflects the "dreaming" of the Aboriginal spiritual beliefs.
- Clap sticks are another favorite instrument.
- Clap sticks are made from hardwood and are tapped together to produce different musical sounds.
- Clap sticks can also be decorated with the Aboriginal designs of the "dreaming."

Clap sticks.

Didgeridoo.

Participants can create didgeridoos and clap sticks as follows.

Materials Needed

Copy of the story *The Singing Snake* by Stefan Czernecki and Timothy Rhodes (New York: Hyperion, 1993).
Paper towel cardboard rolls
Large tongue depressors or craft sticks
Markers, crayons
Transparent tape
White drawing paper

Directions for Participants

Read the story *The Singing Snake* alone, or with a parent or friend.
Make a didgeridoo and a set of clap sticks:
Take 2 cardboard rolls.
Tape the 2 rolls together to create one long roll.
Take some white paper and draw some Aboriginal-type art.
Decorate the roll by covering it with the drawn art.
Take 2 craft sticks and decorate them with some Aboriginal type art using the markers or crayons.
Use the books on display to help you create your artwork.
Play your instruments when you are finished.
Blow a sound through your didgeridoo and clap your sticks together in a rhythmic beat.

An alternative type of Aboriginal Art is Dot Painting.
This can be done by using cotton swabs dipped into paint. Outlines of Australian animals such as Kangaroos and Koalas may be filled in this way. A wonderful example of this can be obtained in the book *World Art: Create Amazing Art with Felt, Foam, and Feathers* by Sue Nicholson (Laguna Hills, CA: QEB

Publishing, 2005). A two-page (pp. 12–13) spread demonstrates a step-by-step approach to Aboriginal painting for children.

Additional adult art books to acquaint you with Aboriginal art include:

Caruana, Wally. 1993. *Aboriginal Art.* New York: Thames and Hudson.
Crumlin, Rosemary, and Anthony Knight. 1991. *Aboriginal Art and Spirituality.* New York: HarperCollins.

INTERACTIVE CENTER 2

BARK PAINTING

The Arnhem Land is known for its old tradition of bark painting. The Aborigines painted on natural surfaces for thousands of years. Rocks, tree bark, and wood were their major surfaces. The paintings tell stories about the land. Artists today still use natural materials, such as bark from eucalyptus trees that is peeled off and dried. The outer portion of the bark is removed and the inner portion is used for the painting. Traditional colors include red, yellow, white, and black paints.

How Participants Can Interact

Use the folktale *Sun Mother Wakes the World* by Diane Wolkstein (see resource list above) as a starting point for children to create their own bark painting of the Australian creation story. You may hang the bark paintings around the display and exhibit area as children create them to establish your own Aboriginal art exhibit.

Bark painting.

Materials Needed

Brown craft paper cut into 9 x 12 inch pieces
Markers or paints in red, yellow, white, and black
and/or chalk in a variety of colors

Directions for Participants

- Read the story *Sun Mother Wakes the World.*
- Take a piece of brown paper and wrinkle it up.

- Smooth out the paper so it looks like eucalyptus bark.
- Using the markers or chalk create a scene from the Australian creation story.

INTERACTIVE CENTER 3
ABORIGINAL STORYTELLING

Stories and myths are the ways Aborigines explain the creation of the world, the land, and the animals, plants, and life around them. Each clan or tribe has their own set of stories and mythical characters, many of them animals such as the Rainbow Serpent or Tiddalik the Frog.

How Participants Can Interact

Several of the stories in the resources mentioned above can be on display. Two in particular may be used for the retelling activity below:
The Biggest Frog in Australia by Susan L. Roth and *Big Rain Coming* by Katerina Germein.

Materials Needed

Sheets of copy paper, white or in pale pastel colors
Crayons, markers, colored pencils

Directions for Participants

Choose a story to read.
Think about how you would retell the story using symbols or pictures only.
Take a sheet of paper and fold it in half lengthwise.
Make an accordion type fold so you have three panels on each side.
Using symbols only, retell the story you read by creating a scene on all six panels.
Color your story when you are finished.
Your story can stand for you to enjoy and retell at home.

Another storytelling resource you may apply to your center is a section on Aborigine Sand Stories in Anne Pellowski's (2005) *Drawing Stories From Around the World*. Westport, CT: Libraries Unlimited.

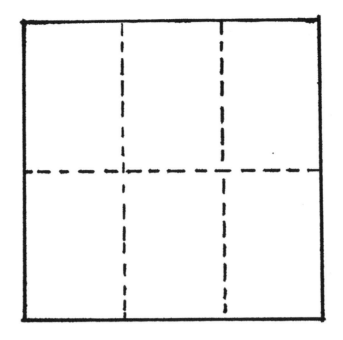

Prefold.

Fold.

Unit 4 Back in Time with Australia's Fascinating History

In this unit, summer readers and their families can discover Captain James Cook and his exploration, Cook's ship the *Endeavour*, the penal colony established by the British, and Australia's Gold Rush, and then create timelines and meet some interesting characters and people with Australian roots.

Resources for This Unit

Blumberg, Rhoda. 1991. *The Remarkable Voyages of Captain Cook.* New York: Bradbury Press.
Boraas, Tracey. 2002. *Australia.* Mankato, MN: Bridgestone Books.
Bruce, Jill B. 1994. *Money of Australia.* 2nd ed. Illustrated by Jan Wade. Victoria, Australia: Kangaroo Press.
Darian-Smith, Kate. 1995. *Exploration into Australia.* New York: New Discovery Books/Simon & Schuster.
Heinrichs, Ann. 1998. *Australia.* New York: Children's Press.
Jordan-Bychkov, Terry G. 2003. *Australia.* Philadelphia: Chelsea House.
Kerns, Ann. 2004. *Australia in Pictures.* Minneapolis: Lerner.

Web Sites

National Library of Australia. http://www.nla.gov.au/pub/endeavour/index.html.
Picture Australia. http://www.pictureaustralia.org/trails_history.html.
   This site offers a "trails tour" of the history through images from a variety of periodical sources.
Time for Kids. Australia Timeline. http://www.timeforkids.com/TFK/hh/goplaces/article/0,20343,485854,00.html.

INTERACTIVE CENTER 1

AUSTRALIA'S TIMELINE OF HISTORY

This center can require a combination of information presented through an exhibit of books, fact charts, and bulletin board displays you may create. The fact charts and bulletin board can point out key historical dates and events that participants can then use to create their timeline. An additional activity may be to create a second historical timeline for the United States so that children may compare and contrast the similarities and differences between the two countries. A surprising amount of parallel events and circumstances can be discovered.

Sample chart for timeline comparison of Australian and U.S. histories:

Australia

1606—Canem Jansz is first European to land in Australia.
1770—Captain James Cook claims the eastern half of Australia as British.
1788—First Fleet of convicts arrives.
1851—Gold is found.

United States

1607—First English settlement in Virginia.
1775—Start of American Revolution.
1789—George Washington is first U.S. president.
1848—Gold is discovered in California.
1861—Civil War begins.

How Participants Can Interact

Using the timeline template, children can write or draw in key historical information based on what they have gleaned from the exhibit. A good book to start with is *Exploration into Australia* by Kate Darian-Smith (see resources list above). In addition, the following three Web sites may be used for families to explore the history online:

Time for Kids Australia Timeline:
http://www.timeforkids.com/TFK/hh/goplaces/article/0,20343,485854,00.html.
Picture Australia offers a "trails tour" of the history through images from a variety of periodical sources:
http://www.pictureaustralia.org/trails_history.html.
United States History Timeline:
http://www.worldalmanacforkids.com/EXPLORE/timeline.html.

Materials Needed

Copies of Australia/United States Timeline template
Pencils, crayons

Directions for Participants

- Create your own timeline with one of the templates.
- Use the books and display to help you decide which events you wish to record.
- Surf through the two timeline Web sites on the computer for additional information.
- You may create a second timeline for the history of the United States.
- How do the two timelines compare? What types of historical events for each country seem similar to you?

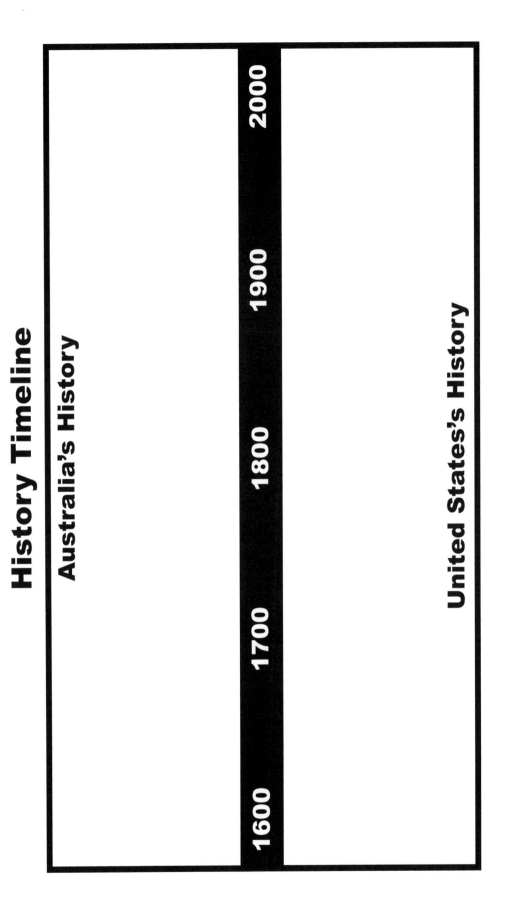

Timeline Markers

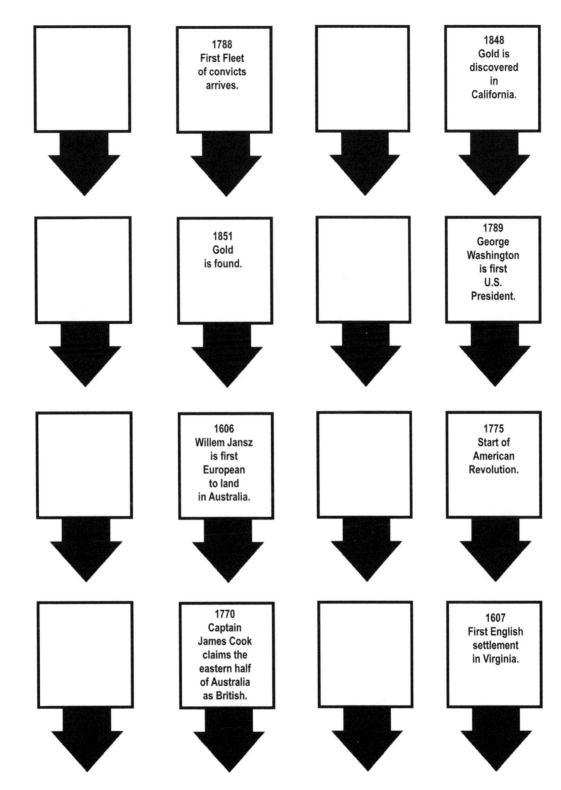

	1788 First Fleet of convicts arrives.		1848 Gold is discovered in California.
	1851 Gold is found.		1789 George Washington is first U.S. President.
	1606 Willem Jansz is first European to land in Australia.		1775 Start of American Revolution.
	1770 Captain James Cook claims the eastern half of Australia as British.		1607 First English settlement in Virginia.

INTERACTIVE CENTER 2

CAPTAIN COOK'S VOYAGE ON THE *ENDEAVOUR*

British explorer James Cook's first remarkable voyage on his ship *Endeavour* included a first look of the "unknown southern continent," the "terra australis incognita." Rhoda Blumberg's wonderfully readable biography, *The Remarkable Voyages of Captain Cook,* can provide some key background information for this center (see resource list above).

How Participants Can Interact

Set up an Internet station to the following Web site, part of the National Library of Australia:

http://www.nla.gov.au/pub/endeavour/teachers/teachers.html#ship.

Viewers can take a virtual trip on a replica of the *Endeavour*, read Captain Cook's journal, and track the path of the voyage.

Tracing Cook's first voyage around the globe and viewing a replica of his ship through the Internet are ways to bring this centuries-old piece of history to life.

Materials Needed

Template of world map (below)
Small rubber stamp of a ship
Colored stamp pads
Pencils or crayons

Directions for Participants

- Take a virtual tour of Captain Cook's voyage on the Internet site.
- When you are finished, mark your map by stamping a ship near each letter.
- Connect the letters to complete Cook's route on his voyage between 1768 and 1771.
- Color your map when finished.

To understand better what life may have been like on board a voyage with Captain Cook, you may include the short and satirical book *You Wouldn't Want to Travel with Captain Cook!: A Voyage You'd Rather Not Make* by Mark Bergin, illustrated by David Antram (New York: Franklin Watts, 2006) and encourage your participants to read it at the center.

Captain Cook's 1770 Voyage

Directions: Connect the letters to complete Captain Cook's 1770 voyage.

INTERACTIVE CENTER 3

BOTANY BAY AND THE CONVICTS

Britain's claim to the "unoccupied" land of Australia resulted in a division of the continent into separate colonies. Some of these colonies, such as Botany Bay, were created as prisoner or penal settlements. Convicts, most of whom had committed minor thefts, were in debt and very poor. They were brought over to these settlements with an average sentence of seven years' hard labor. Transport of convicts lasted from 1788 through 1868.

How Participants Can Interact

The short, satirical look at a convict's life en route to Botany Bay can be explained in *You Wouldn't Want to Be an 18th-Century British Convict!: A Trip to Australia You'd Rather Not Take* by Meredith Costain, illustrated by David Antram (New York: Franklin Watts, 2007). Families can read this book together, discuss, and use some of the other history books mentioned in the resources for further information. A word search using vocabulary in the book and glossary can be created to have available as a follow-up.

Materials Needed

Copies of book as mentioned above
Copies of word search
Pencils

INTERACTIVE CENTER 4

FAMOUS AUSTRALIANS—WHO ARE THEY?

Biographical information can be displayed at this center with books from your collection or with brief fact sheets about some less well-known yet important figures in Australia's history. A good source for this is the book *Money of Australia* by Jill B. Bruce (see reference list above), which provides both historical events and famous people that are commemorated in Australia's currency.

How Participants Can Interact

Based on information presented throughout this unit and center, you can create a matching board from the list of people and their accomplishment or reason for recognition. You may add names as you wish. In addition, a handout sheet with the same matching information can be prepared.

Penal Colony of Australia
WORD SEARCH

FLOGGING	CHAIN GANG	HARD LABOR	SENTENCE
DETERRENT	FENCE	EXILE	BEADLE
PETITION	CONVICT	ENCLOSURE ACTS	TYPHUS
STOCKS	OLD BAILEY	TREADMILL	TICKET OF LEAVE
COLONY	HULKS	GALLOWS	PUNISHMENT
CRIME	SCURVY	HIGHWAYMAN	

```
K A M C V T Y S D W O I L L S E N T E N C E
C O N V I C T S T H P L Q M C V W Q N Z P P
H R I N R F L O G G I N G Y U S Y X C M U S
A I I P O E S K X M Q U D W R X N I L B N K
R T J M O N R I D S R E Z Z V D O A O D I E
D H A A E C O A U Y T T D P Y M L A S L S S
L U H S A E E N O I T I T E P D O B U K H F
A L H T H R P X S A I Y M H A L C P R X M C
B K L O T A A M I C C U L C L O X T E P E E
O S N C M Y Z P O L K Q W H O O Z S A X N P
R D A K X D P O W M E L D A E B A S C T T A
A H A S V T R H L O T Y V I I R R O T S L L
X C A A S U I K U U O U M N N S X I S A P P
T N E R R E T E D S F X N G G O W S B O U O
K L M O U V Y R W O L E P A L M A O C Z E E
C S U R R Y O O D Q E C A N M M I X L L O U
D E H I G H W A Y M A N K G E O O K J L W E
E T E R R S W A A Z V J L T Y F E S S R A O
J U S W R C E S S Y E L I A B D L O G C D G
```

Penal Colony of Australia
ANSWERS

Materials Needed

Large magnetic board
Index cards in two or three colors
Magnetic stick-on strips

Creating Your Matching Board

- Write the name of each figure on a separate index card.
- Write the accompanying accomplishment on a different index card.
- Laminating the cards can help your center be more durable.
- Cut magnetic strips to fit the cards and peel and stick on the back.
- Have the two sets of cards (people and accomplishments) scrambled in a box.
- Allow participants to unscramble and place matching cards on the magnetic board.

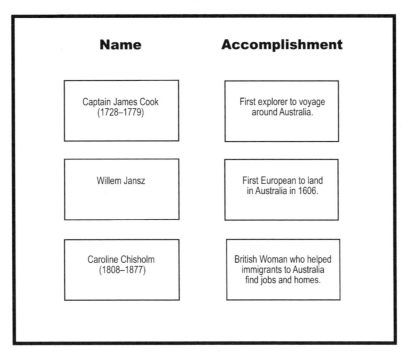

Matching Board Game.

- Joseph Banks (1743–1820)
- Botanist who traveled with Captain Cook.
- John MacArthur (1767–1834)
- British officer who began Australia's sheep and wool industry.
- Willem Jansz
- First European to land in Australia in 1606.
- Caroline Chisholm (1808–1877)
- British woman who helped female immigrants to Australia find jobs and homes.
- Captain James Cook (1728–1779)
- First explorer to voyage around Australia.
- Robert O'Hara Burke (1820–1861) and John Wills (1834–1861)
- First Europeans to cross Australia from north to south in 1860.

		Henry Lawson (1867–1922)
	Francis Greenaway (1777–1837)	Poet and short-story writer.
William Farrer (1845–1906)	Australia's first architect. Arrived as a convict for forgery and the only convict to appear on a banknote.	
English farmer who experimented with breeding varieties of wheat in Australia.	Lord Howard Florey (1898–1968) and Sir Alexander Fleming	Victor Chang (1936–1991)
Sir Charles Kingsford Smith (1897–1935)	Developed the life-saving drug penicillin.	Cardiac surgeon and pioneer of the modern era of heart transplantation.
Australia's greatest pioneer aviator. Made the first flight across the Pacific Ocean from the U.S. to Australia in 1928.		

Evonne Goolagong Cawley (1951–)	Cathy Freeman (1973–)	Pearl Gibbs (1901–1983)	
Tennis champion and winner of seven Grand Slam Tournaments.	First Aborigine to win an Olympic gold medal for the 400-meter race in Sydney in 2000.	Aborigine active in the Aboriginal rights movement and called the "mother of reconciliation."	
Eddie Mabo (1936–1992)			
Organized and led the battle to change the law of" terra nullius" (British claim to undeclared land). He is responsible for the High Court of Australia overturning "terra nullius" in 1992, now known as the historic Mabo Decision.			

Add Pizzazz to Summer Down Under: An Awesome Aussie Experience

During portions of the two-week unit periods, event programming can be planned to include any of the following ideas:

Arvo Tea and Storytelling Hour

Hire a professional storyteller for this family event or, just as effectively, develop a read-aloud story-hour session by a staff librarian. Food chosen from the Arvo recipes may be prepared and served.

Strine Charades Competition

Set up a family program night and divide parents and children into multi-age teams. Use the strine vocabulary to create charade challenges.

Australian Geography Bee

Explore some official Geography Bee Web sites such as

National Geographic GeoBee Challenge
http://www.nationalgeographic.com/geobee/ or
Geography Quizzes: The Australia Quiz
http://www.lizardpoint.com/fun/geoquiz/ausquiz.html

to develop questions that can be offered throughout your first unit on a PowerPoint-style presentation. Follow through with an official contest program on a designated afternoon or evening.

Aussie Animal-Petting Program

Cooperate with your local zoo to see if they provide a traveling animal science program that might include one or two native Australian critters families can experience and learn about in a live format.

Aborigine Actuality Tournament

Much like a chess tournament, reproduce several copies of the game to offer a challenging evening of competition and fun.

Aboriginal Arts Museum Exhibition Opening

Hold an official art exhibit opening with fancy treats and an official looking artists' program brochure for your young patrons' artwork.

Captain Cook Treasure Hunt

The three main voyages of Captain Cook's exploration left a legacy of discoveries. Create a hunt through the library with clues for several of the most famous, such as the discovery of the Sandwich Islands now known as Hawaii, the development of longitude, botanical discovery of new plants, and others.

Annotated Bibliography of Australian-Related Fiction

Base, Graeme. 1998. *My Grandma Lived in Gooligulch.* Davis, CA: The Australian Book Source. Grades K–3.

> In this rhyming illustrated poem story, the ever-resourceful Grandma introduces us to a menagerie of Australian animals from the koala to the lyrebird.

Bateson, Catherine. 2005. *Stranded in Boringsville.* New York: Holiday House. Grades 4–6.

> After the divorce, Rain May and her mother move to "Boringsville," the tiny town of Clarkston in Central Victoria, where life is simpler yet adjustments to a new school and friends still need to be made. The Australian setting offers some city/country differences between Melbourne and Clarkson.

Beatty, Patricia. 1982. *Jonathan Down Under.* New York: William Morrow.

> This Australian pioneer gold-rush story takes thirteen-year-old Jonathan Cole and his prospector father from California to the rousing adventurous mining camp called Ballarat in nineteenth-century Victoria.

Carmi, Rebecca. 2002. *Expedition Down Under.* Illustrations by John Speirs. A Magic School Bus Chapter Book. New York: Scholastic Paperbacks. Grades 2–4.

> Ms. Frizzle's class takes a trip to the outback on the other side of the world where they search for a kookaburra, race a herd of kangaroos, and survive a run-in with a Tasmanian Devil.

Cohn, Rachel. 2003. *The Steps.* New York: Simon & Schuster. Grades 5–8.

> New Yorker Annabel travels to Sidney, Australia, to visit and become acquainted with her newly remarried father's wife, Penny, and stepchildren, Angus and Lucy. Annabel's adjustment to her new Australian instant family involves learning about her new stepsiblings in addition to a whole new way of life.

Elmer, Robert. *Adventures Down Under* (series running between 1997–99). Minneapolis: Bethany House. Grades 4–6.

> Action-packed mysteries involving Patrick McWaid and his family, who have followed their father to a penal colony in Australia and attempt to clear his unjustified arrest.

French, Jackie. 1999. *Hitler's Daughter.* New York: HarperCollins. Grades 5–7.

> While waiting for the school bus each day during the incessant rains, some contemporary Australian children listen to a story their friend Heidi is developing. What if Hitler had a daughter who was disabled and he kept hidden? As details unfold each day, the story prompts ethical questions about genocide, the treatment of the Aboriginal people, and war in general.

Herrick, Steven. 2006. *By the River.* Asheville, NC: Front Street. Grades 5–7.

> Set in a small Australian town in 1962, 14-year-old Harry Hodby fantasizes about leaving this rural river town but is haunted by memories of losing his mother in the seasonal floods. Rich free-verse poetic narration by one of Australia's top poets.

Hesse, Karen. 2000. *Stowaway.* Illustrated Robert Andrew Parker. New York: Margaret K. McElderry. Grades 4–6.

> In the summer of 1768, 11-year-old orphan Nicholas Young sneaks aboard the *H.M.S. Endeavour* to escape his brutal life as the butcher's apprentice, hoping to discover adven-

ture and a new life on the "unknown continent" called Australia. An historical fictional account told in diary format.

Hill, Anthony. 1995. *The Burnt Stick.* Boston, MA: Houghton Mifflin. Grades 5–7.

When John Jagamarra was only five years old, he was taken to a mission school to be raised in the ways of the white people. Born to an Aborigine mother and white father, John was forced to leave his Aboriginal home to obey the laws created by the white European settlers.

Hirsch, Odo. 2006. *Something's Fishy, Hazel Green.* New York: Bloomsbury. Grades 4–6.

Australian character Hazel Green returns to solve a mystery for the fishmonger, Mr. Petrusca, who has had his prize lobsters stolen and is reluctant to reveal he cannot read the nonsensical note left by the thief. Hazel settles in to solve both problems, finding the thief and helping Mr. Petrusca solve his reading issue in her determinedly good-hearted way.

Marsden, John. 1994. *Dead of night.* Boston, MA: Houghton. Grades 5–7.

———. 1995. *Tomorrow, When the War Began.* Boston, MA: Houghton.

The first two books in the Tomorrow adventure series, which is about teenagers involved in a struggle to help free their country from an invading foreign military force in league with a band of disaffected Australians. Returning from a camping trip, Ellie and her friends find their homes burned or deserted, their families imprisoned, and their country occupied. The series continues with *Killing Frost* (1995), *Darkness Be My Friend* (1996), *Burning for Revenge* (2000), *Night Is for Hunting* (2001), and *The Other Side of Dawn* (2002).

Osborne, Mary Pope. 2000. *Dingoes at Dinnertime.* Illustrated by Sal Murdocca. A Magic Tree House Book. New York: Random House. Grades 3–4.

Jack and his sister Annie have traveled to Australia and must save a host of animals from a raging wildfire during a drought.

Stanley, George Edward. 2004. *Adam Sharp: Code Word Kangaroo.* Illustrated by Guy Francis. A Stepping Stone Book. New York: Random House. Grades 2–3.

Superspy Adam Sharp goes to Australia to track down the evildoer who has blocked all T.V. stations except "the Happy Channel."

Zindel, Paul. 1998. *Reef of Death.* New York: HarperCollins. Grades 5–7.

This thrilling adventure set in the exotic Australian Great Barrier Reef involves Maruul, an Aboriginal girl, and P. C. McPhee, an American friend, who work to save the village from the evil plotting Dr. Ecenbarger, a German scientist, who is running an illegal undersea operation.

8

The Invention Convention

Outline of Program

Weeks 1 & 2—Ancient History
1. Tools
2. Art
3. The Wheel
4. Numbers/Math

Weeks 3 & 4—Inventions That Changed Our World
1. Farming
2. Industrial technology
3. Communication

Weeks 5 & 6—The Inventor's Hall of Fame
1. Focus on Galileo, Edison, da Vinci
2. Memory Game

Weeks 7 & 8—Be Your Own Inventor
1. Displays created by participants
2. "Invention Convention" open house

Since humanity's early beginnings, ways to make life easier and more productive have developed and evolved—from simple hand tools to modern day science and technology. You can create a summer-long interactive reading program drawing from a variety of subjects across your collection to include prehistoric discoveries, ancient science and mathematics, communication through art, industrial innovations, brilliant or accidental inventors through the years, and even offer an opportunity to hold your own invention convention in your community. Four units with themes and exhibits can be organized as follows.

Invention Convention
Game Sheet

Ask a librarian to stamp your game sheet
with an "idea light bulb" for every box you complete.

Attend a Program	Read for One Hour	Read about an Inventor	Read for One Hour	Attend a Program
Read for 1/2 Hour	Poetry Potpourri (Read a Book of Poems)	Finish an Invention Interactive Center	Find the Dewey Number for Books on Inventions	Read for 1/2 Hour
Read for One Hour	Find the Dewey Number for Your Favorite Invention	Attend the Open House Kickoff	Read a Fairytale or a Picture Book	Read for One Hour
Read for 1/2 Hour	Finish an Invention Interactive Center	Read a Short Story	Finish an Invention Interactive Center	Read for 1/2 Hour
Attend a Program	Read for One Hour	Finish an Invention Interactive Center	Read for One Hour	Attend a Program

5 **Boxes Stamped = Your Name on the Idea Board**

10 **Boxes Stamped = Your Name on the Design Board**

15 **Boxes Stamped = Your Name on a Inventor's Certificate**

From *Summer Reading Renaissance: An Interactive Exhibits Approach* by Rita Soltan. Illustrations by Jill Reichenbach Fill. Westport, CT: Libraries Unlimited. Copyright © 2008.

Invention Convention
Summary Reading Program

- Register.

- Read-to-Me to Grade 8 may participate.

- Take your reading game sheet home and READ, READ, READ! Keep track of the time you spend reading.

- Participate in our interactive centers and attend library programs!

- When you've completed a box on your game sheet, ask a librarian to stamp the appropriate box.

- Complete 5 boxes — put your name on the Idea Board.

- Complete 10 boxes — put your name on the Design Board.

- Complete 15 boxes — receive an Inventor's Certificate, Books, or a coupon.

- Complete all boxes — receive an entry in the Grand Prize Drawing!

- The LAST DAY to have game sheets stamped is _____.

- Enter the weekly lotto each time you visit the library (one entry per day) for a chance to win a _____. You must be registered in Summer Reading to enter.

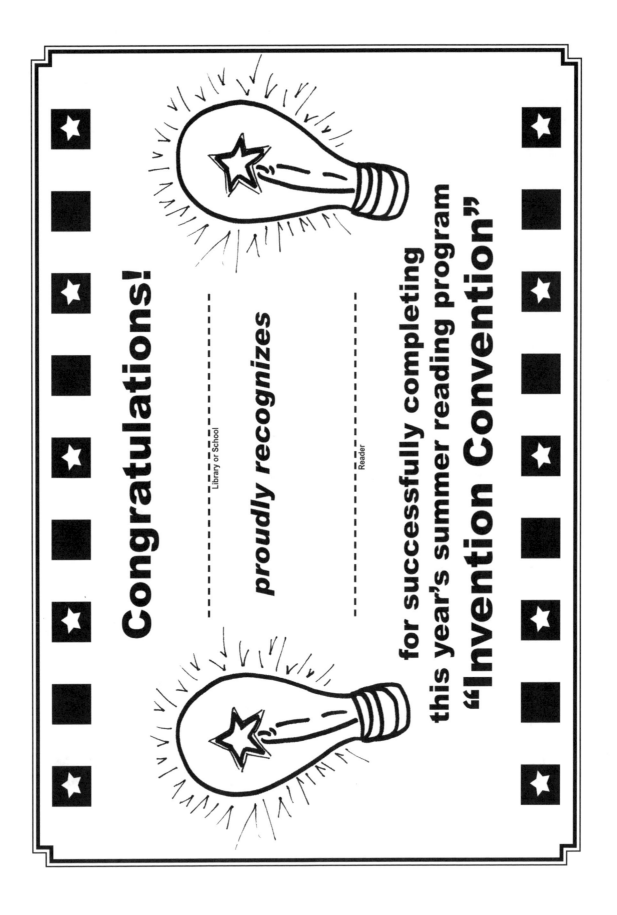

Congratulations!

Library or School

proudly recognizes

Reader

for successfully completing
this year's summer reading program
"Invention Convention"

Unit 1 Necessary Beginnings

Introduce this summer-long theme with some of the first important inventions.

- the use of stone tools, which led to stone hand axes, spears, arrow points, and sickles—the forerunners of screwdrivers, chisels, and kitchen knives
- the development of the wheel and the axle
- communication through various forms of art, language, and writing
- a system of counting and figuring in units of ten

Resources for This Unit

Bailey, Gerry. 2003. *First Thousand Years.* Illustrated by Steve Boulter and Jan Smith. Minneapolis, MN: Picture Window Books.

———. 2003. *Long, Long, Ago.* Illustrated by Steve Boulter and Jan Smith. Minneapolis, MN: Picture Window Books.

———. 2003. *Early Civilizations.* Illustrated by Steve Boulter and Jan Smith. Minneapolis, MN: Picture Window Books.

Bender, Lionel. 2005. *Invention.* Rev. ed. Illustrated by Dave King. New York and London: DK Publishing.

Bridgeman, Roger Francis. 2006. *1,000 Inventions and Discoveries.* New York and London: DK Publishing.

Haven, Kendall. 2006. *100 Greatest Science Inventions of All Time.* Westport, CT: Libraries Unlimited.

———. 2007. *100 Greatest Science Discoveries of All Time.* Westport, CT: Libraries Unlimited.

Sachs, Jessica Snyder. 2001. *The Encyclopedia of Inventions.* New York: Franklin Watts.

Tomecek, Stephen M. 2003. *What A Great Idea! Inventions That Changed the World.* Illustrated by Dan Stuckenschneider. New York: Scholastic.

Web Sites

Museum of Ancient Inventions. http://www.smith.edu/hsc/museum/ancient_inventions/home.htm.

INTERACTIVE CENTER 1

STONE AGE TOOLS

They say that "necessity is the mother of invention," and in prehistoric times the need to extend humanity's capabilities with the use of hands led to the invention of simple pebble tools—the hand ax, the spear, and arrow points—to facilitate foraging and hunting for food.

Set up an Internet station to the following Web site:

The Museum of Antiquities, Newcastle University, UK

http://museums.ncl.ac.uk/flint/menu.html.

Participants can work their way through the various links to learn about the Stone Age hunter and his tools.

You may also wish to create a portable bulletin board exhibit from resources on prehistoric books and tools in your collection and the books suggested below.

A Stone Age Tool Set

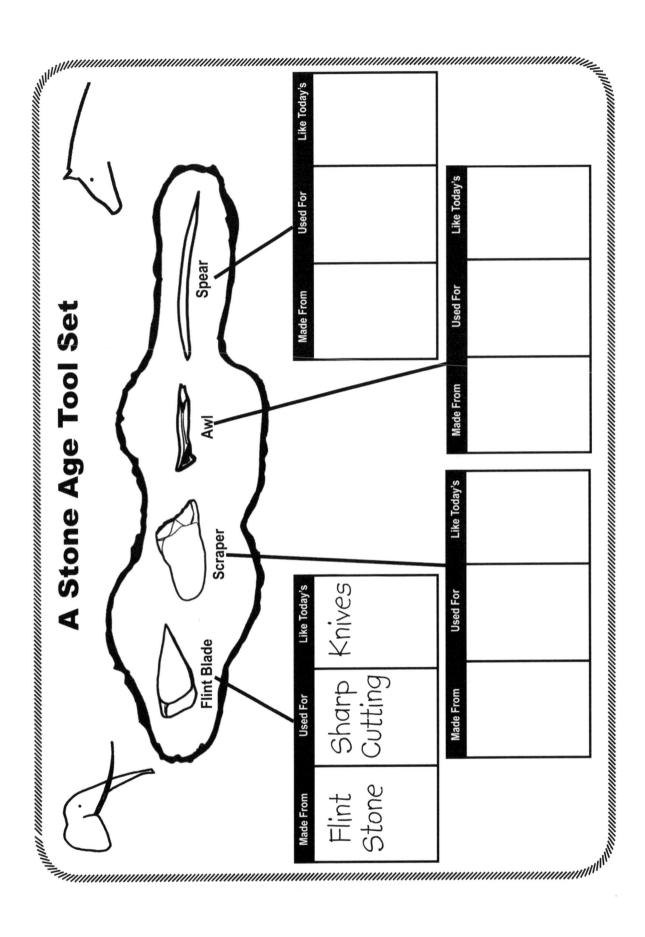

Spear

Awl

Scraper

Flint Blade

Made From	Used For	Like Today's

Made From	Used For	Like Today's

Made From	Used For	Like Today's

Made From	Used For	Like Today's
Flint Stone	Sharp Cutting	Knives

Materials Needed

Reproducible sheet for: A Stone Age Tool Set
Crayons, colored pencils

Books on Display

Facchini, Fiorenzo. 2003. *A Day with Neanderthal Man.* Brookfield, CT: Twenty First Century Books.
  Pages 28–32 simply and clearly outline a "workshop" for this time period.
Hayward, Linda. 1997. *Cave People.* New York: Grosset & Dunlap.
Hynes, Margaret. 2003. *The Best Book of Early People.* New York: Kingfisher.
  Pages 10–13 have excellent large drawings of early tools.
Macdonald, Fiona. 1998. *The Stone Age News.* New York: Walker.
  Includes a very visual two-page spread (pp. 16–17) on tools and how they might have been made.
Mason, Anthony. 1996. *The Time Trekkers Visit the Stone Age.* Illustrated by Sheena Vickers. Brookfield, CT: Copper Beech Books.

Both younger and older children can easily make comparisons between prehistoric and modern-day tools with the following picture-oriented books:

Gibbons, Gail. 1982. *The Tool Book.* New York: Holiday House.
Morris, Ann. 1992. *Tools.* Photographs by Ken Heyman. New York: Lothrop, Lee & Shepard.
Robbins, Ken. 1983. *Tools.* New York: Four Winds Press.
Rockwell, Anne. 2004. *The Toolbox.* New York: Walker.
Shulman, Lisa. 2002. *Old Macdonald Had a Woodshop.* Illustrations by Ashley Wolff. New York: G. P. Putnam's.
Singer, Marilyn. 2006. *Let's Build a Clubhouse.* Illustrations by Timothy Bush. New York: Clarion.
Sturges, Philemon. 2006. *I Love Tools!* New York: HarperCollins.

How Participants Can Interact

Parents and children can use the resources provided through the bulletin board exhibit, Internet station, and the reading of the books on display to learn about Stone Age tools. They can then fill in some of their findings on the reproducible sheet including their comparisons with prehistoric and modern day tools.

Directions for Participants

- Use the display, the Internet computer station, and the books to learn about tools used in the Stone Age.
- Read some of the books at the table alone, or with a parent or friend.
- Find the information given about Stone Age tools.
- Record what you know or have learned about each kind of tool on the Tool Set sheet.
- Read some of the modern tool books on display.

- What modern tools can you compare with the Stone Age tools? Record them on your sheet.
- Color in your sheet and information as you wish.

INTERACTIVE CENTER 2

CAVE PAINTING

Early artists used natural materials to create paints and brushes. Minerals in the soil and rocks were used as powdered paints; chalk was used as a white powder, and charcoal as black. The powder was applied to wet rocks or sometimes mixed with oil (animal fat) to make it stick to a hide or bone surface. The powdered paint is thought to have been kept in hollow tubes made from animal bones. Paintings were often of animals, but hands were used as stencils against a rock or cave wall and the powdered paint was applied around them. Hands represented an important symbol since prehistoric people could make tools, other objects of necessity such as clothing, and communicate through sign language, all with their hands.

Cave Hand Prints

Hand cave painting.

Materials Needed

Brown 8 x 10 inch craft paper sheets
Colored sand in browns, reds, white, black
Small paper cups to hold sand
Large cookie tray for extra sand (as tray fills you may reuse multi-colors in extra paper cups)
Glue sticks or white glue and cotton swabs (messy hands can be cleaned up by providing a supply of inexpensive hand wipes or encourage a trip to the lavatory)

Books on Display

Hodge, Susie. 1998. *Prehistoric Art*. Des Plaines, IL: Heinemann Interactive Library.
Hynes, Margaret. 2003. *The Best Book of Early People*. New York: Kingfisher, pp. 18–19.

Web Sites to Include on an Internet Station

The Cave of Lascaux (in France):
    French Ministry of Culture and Communication
    http://www.culture.gouv.fr/culture/arcnat/lascaux/en/.
Harcourt School Publishers. A Virtual Tour of Cave Painting.
    http://www.hbschool.com/activity/cavepaintings/vallon.html.

How Participants Can Interact

Using the books and Web sites as a reference, children can recreate a cave hand print.

Directions for Participants

- Take a piece of brown paper and crumple it.
- Open the paper and smooth it out a bit.
- Using a glue stick or a cotton swab filled with glue, trace your hand on the paper.
- Choose two sand cups with different colors.
- Sprinkle the sand over the glue tracing of your hand.
- Let your painting dry.
- Sift the extra sand onto the cookie tray.
- Your cave hand print is ready to hang on the wall!

INTERACTIVE CENTER 3

WHEELS GO ROUND AND ROUND

When humans realized that a rolling log could move downhill with the force of gravity and not just with human power, the concept of the wheel was born. The wheel is one of the most important inventions of humankind as it led to the development of numerous other forms of machines to help humans with their work, beyond just the use of strong animals.

Books on Display

Glover, David. 2006. *Wheels and Cranks.* Chicago: Heinemann Library.
Locke, Ian. 1995. *The Wheel and How It Changed the World.* New York: Facts on File.
Pipe, Jim. 2002. *What Does a Wheel Do?* New York: Copper Beach Books.
Randolph, Joanne. 2006. *Wheels and Axles in My World.* New York: PowerKids Press.
Scarry, Huck. 1980. *On Wheels.* New York: Philomel Books.
Tiner, John Hudson. 2003. *Wheels and Axles.* North Mankato, MN: Smart Apple Media.
Welsbacher, Anne. 2001. *Wheels and Axles.* Mankato, MN. Bridgestone Books.
Zubrowski, Bernie. 1986. *Wheels at Work.* New York: William Morrow.

Materials Needed

Large, heavyweight or dictionary-sized book
6–8 round unsharpened pencils

How Participants Can Interact

The concept of rolling to move heavy objects can be demonstrated at this center. Children can see how the use of rollers, simulating the first logs used by early humans, achieved momentum and made the movement of heavy objects easier through the force of gravity rather than just human strength. The third experiment illustrates how to move objects more effectively over an uneven surface.

Book experiment.

Directions for Participants

- Take the large book and place it directly on the table.
- Push the book with one hand. Note how hard your hand must push to move the book.
- Place 6 pencils evenly spaced under the book.
- Push the book over the pencils with one hand. What happens? What is different?
- Add 2 pencils under the 6 pencils at a right angle.
- Push the book over the pencils with one hand. What happens? What is different?
- Why would it be good to use the 2 pencils under the 6 pencils to roll the book?

Directions

- Look at some of the books on display.
- How many different ways do we use wheels today?
- List your ideas on the "Wheels Go Round and Round" sheet.

Wheels Go Round and Round

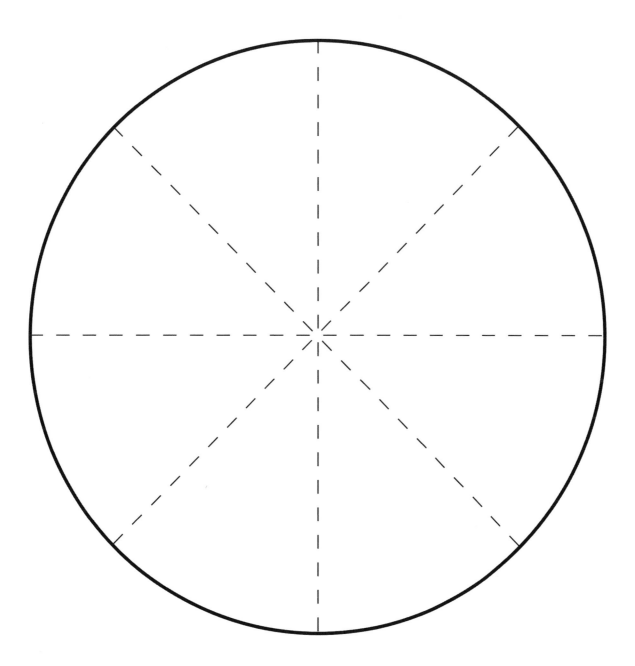

INTERACTIVE CENTER 4

NUMBERS AND THE MANY WAYS TO COUNT

Early humans began to use a system of counting by making rows of tally marks or tying knots in cords. Early counting may also have been based on the use of 10 fingers and 10 toes. Counting led to the development of different systems of symbols used to record and represent the number of things.

Books on Display

Downey, Tika. 2004. *The History of Zero.* New York: Rosen Publishing.
Faiella, Graham. 2006. *The Technology of Mesopotamia.* New York: Rosen Publishing.
Fisher, Leonard Everett. 1982. *Number Art: Thirteen 123s from Around the World.* New York: Four Winds Press.
Ganeri, Anita. 1996. *The Story of Numbers and Counting.* New York: Oxford University Press.
Schmandt-Besserat, Denis. 1999. *The History of Counting.* Illustrated by Michael Hays. New York: Morrow Junior Books.
Woods, Mary B. and Michael. 2000. *Ancient Computing from Counting to Calendars.* Minneapolis, MN: Runestone Press.

How Participants Can Interact

The various ways of counting and working with numbers can be demonstrated through three different activities. Magic squares, developed in ancient China, enable children to work through and create a number puzzle. The use of a Chinese abacus to count can also be employed. Finally, the board game mancala uses a number and counting system that is thought to have been the forerunner of the abacus.

Children can begin this center by reading the book *Fun With Numbers* by Massin (New York: Harcourt, Brace, 1995) to get an overview of how the use of numbers began and the many ways of counting and measuring developed.

Magic Squares

This is an addition or subtraction activity that requires some basic arithmetic skills.

Materials Needed

Books:

Adams, Colleen. 2006. *Magic Squares.* New York: Rosen.
Murphy, Frank. 2001. *Ben Franklin and the Magic Squares.* Illustrated by Richard Walz. New York: Random House.
Magic Squares sheet

Magic Squares 3x3

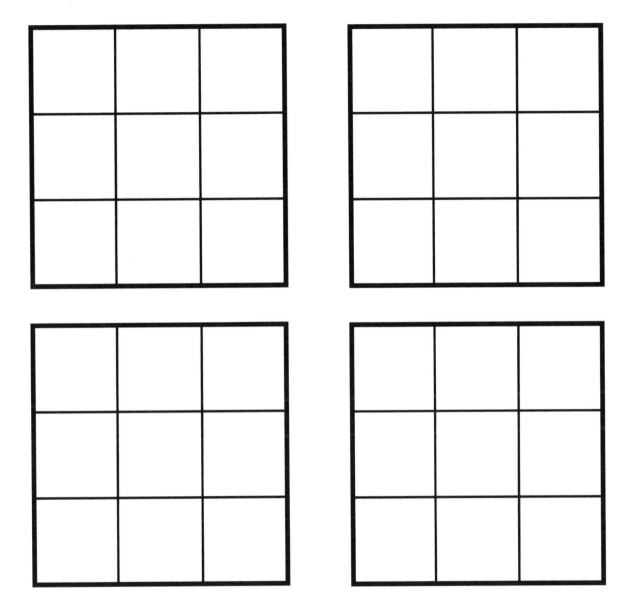

Magic Squares 4x4

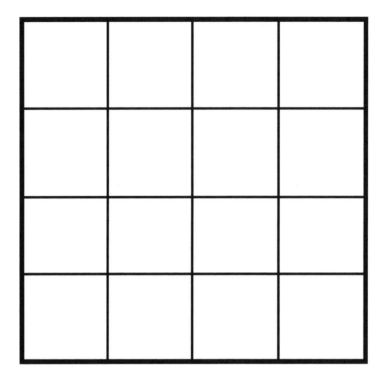

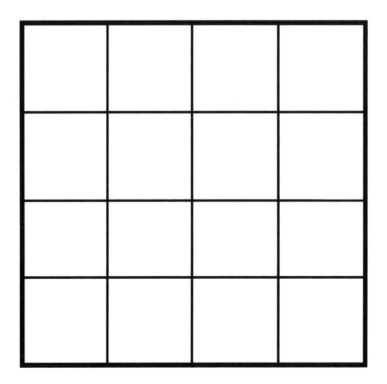

Directions for Participants

- Read the two books about magic squares by yourself, with a friend, or with a parent.
- Follow the directions at the back of the Ben Franklin book (pp. 45–47) to create your own magic squares.
- How many versions can you come up with?

A good Internet resource to help create other magic square activities for this center can be found at http://mathforum.org/alejandre/magic.square.html, part of Drexel University's School of Education.

Counting with an Abacus

Abacus.

Book:

Pilegard, Virginia Walton. 2001. *The Warlord's Beads.* Gretna, LA: Pelican Publishing.

Materials Needed

An inexpensive toy abacus may be provided or, after reading the story, children can create their own following the directions at the back of Pilegard's book using cardboard, pipe cleaners, and toasted oats cereal.

A good Web site to provide ways of counting and doing math with an abacus can be found at http://nlvm.usu.edu/en/nav/frames_asid_196_g_3_t_1.html, part of the National Library of Virtual Manipulatives at Utah State University.

Mancala

A couple of inexpensive mancala sets may be available at this center or children can make their own with the following materials.

Materials Needed

Egg carton
48 kidney or lima beans
2 bathroom-size cups

Directions for Participants

- Cut the top off the egg carton, leaving the 12 egg cups.
- Place a paper cup at either end of the egg cups.
- Set up the mancala game with 4 beans in each egg cup.

Book to help with mancala rules and strategies:

King, Daniel. 2003. *Games: Learn to Play, Play to Win.* New York: Kingfisher, pp. 30–32.

You might also set up a computer station with a CD-ROM version of mancala such as: Bicycle Board Games: 16 of Your Favorite Board Games (Microsoft, 2003).

Unit 2 Inventions That Changed Our World

The plethora of choices for this unit offers numerous ideas but can also present an overwhelming area for display and interactive centers. For this reason, it would make sense to work from three broad groups.

- farming and agriculture created new ways for humans to feed themselves and created a market economy
- industrial technology allowed for production and manufacturing to develop and expand
- communication cultivated a way for people to be in contact with others beyond their small village and widened to a worldwide level of information and resources

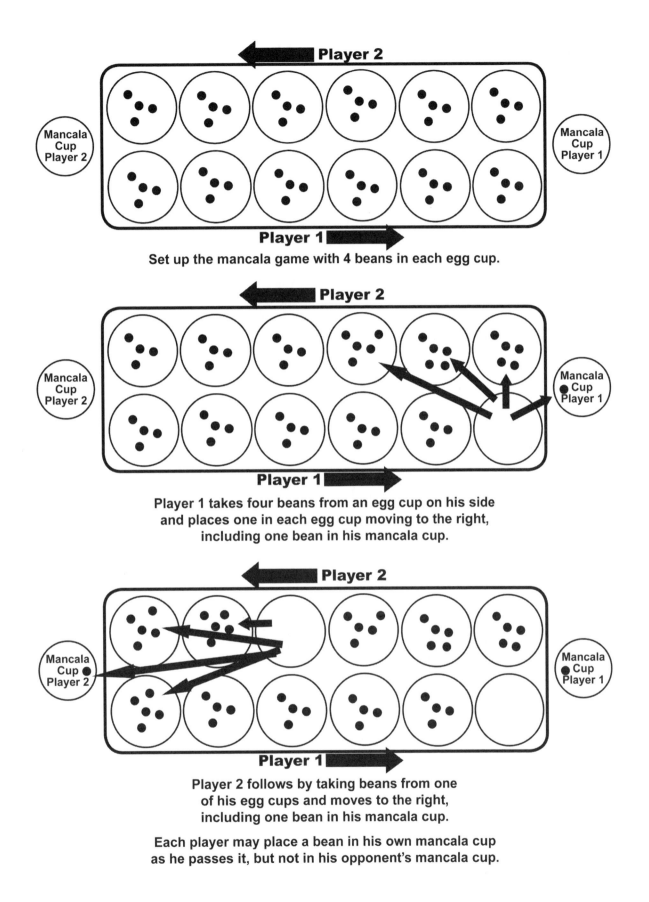

Player 2

Player 1

Set up the mancala game with 4 beans in each egg cup.

Player 2

Player 1

Player 1 takes four beans from an egg cup on his side
and places one in each egg cup moving to the right,
including one bean in his mancala cup.

Player 2

Player 1

Player 2 follows by taking beans from one
of his egg cups and moves to the right,
including one bean in his mancala cup.

Each player may place a bean in his own mancala cup
as he passes it, but not in his opponent's mancala cup.

How to Play Mancala

- Two players face each other with 6 egg cups for each player and one paper cup, called the mancala cup, to each player's right.
- Players take turns placing one bean successively in each cup, moving to the right.
- Player 1 takes four beans from an egg cup on his side and places one in each egg cup moving to the right.
- Player 2 follows by taking beans from one of his egg cups and moving to the right, dropping a bean in his mancala cup when appropriate.
- Each player may place a bean in his own mancala cup as he passes it, but not in his opponent's mancala cup.
- If a player uses his last bean in his own mancala cup, he may take another turn.
- When one of the players uses his last bean, the game ends. If a player drops his last bean in one of his empty cups, he may take all the beans in the opposite cup as well. The winner is the player with the most beans.

From *Summer Reading Renaissance: An Interactive Exhibits Approach* by Rita Soltan. Illustrations by Jill Reichenbach Fill. Westport, CT: Libraries Unlimited. Copyright © 2008.

Each of these broad groups can be represented with any number of center topics. Below is a sampling of what might be created. The resources provided can help you expand or recreate other centers as you deem appropriate and feasible for your library. You may do one from each center for a week or rotate over a longer period.

Resources for This Unit

Bender, Lionel. 2005. *Invention*. Rev. ed. Illustrated by Dave King. New York and London: DK Publishers.

Parker, Steve. 1992. *53 1/2 Things That Changed the World and Some That Didn't*. Brookfield, CN: Millbrook.

Platt, Richard. 2003. *Eureka! Great Inventions and How They Happened*. Boston: Kingfisher.

Tomecek, Stephen M. 2003. *What a Great Idea! Inventions That Changed the World*. Illustrated by Dan Stuckenschneider. New York: Scholastic.

Williams, Marcia. 2005. *Hooray for Inventors!* Cambridge, MA: Candlewick.

In addition, two wonderful resources to help you create other centers involving early and modern technology are the following books:

Edom, Helen, and Kate Woodward. 1992. *The Usborne Book of Science Activities*. Vol. 1. London: Usborne.

Kassinger, Ruth. 2001. *Reinvent the Wheel: Make Classic Inventions, Discover Your Problem-Solving Genius, and Take the Inventor's Challenge*. New York: John Wiley.

INTERACTIVE CENTER 1

FARMING THEN AND NOW

How Participants Can Interact

Farming was one of the initial ways humans learned to feed themselves beyond the primitive methods of foraging and hunting. Farming allowed people to create more stable communities and eventually grew to one of the first elements of a trading society. Children and adults can create their own "concept barn" of information through reading books and exploring certain museum-oriented Web sites to learn and record some of the ways farming developed and changed.

Set up an Internet station with the web address of Living History Farms: http://www.lhf.org/farmsites.html.

This site allows exploration of farming techniques used by the Ioway Indians, two Iowa farms before and after the Civil War period, and a horse-powered farm from the early 1900s.

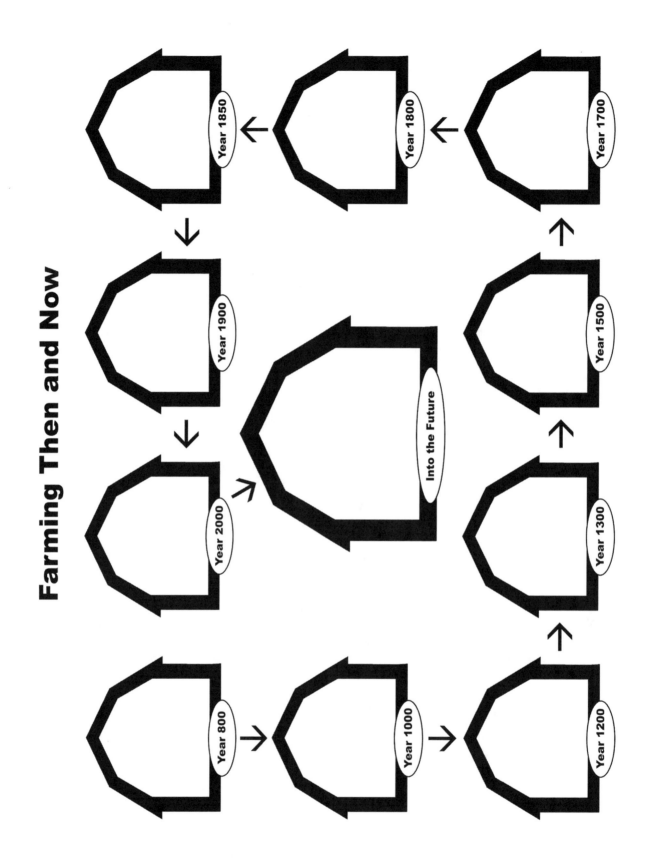

Farming Then and Now

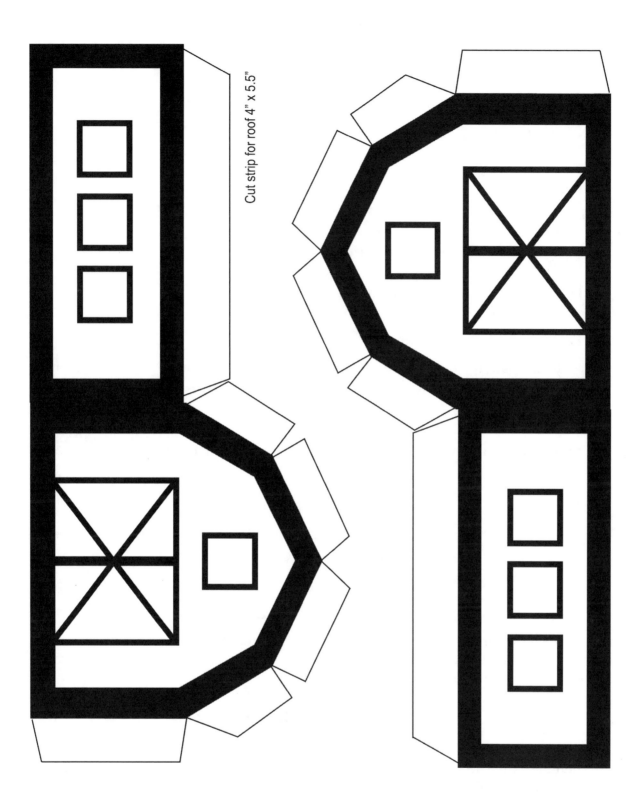

Cut strip for roof 4" x 5.5"

Materials Needed

Barn concept web sheet
Paper barn pattern
Pencils, crayons, markers
Books for older children:

Chrisp, Peter. 1993. *The Farmer through History.* Illustrated by Tony Smith. New York: Thomson Learning.
Wilkes, Angela. 2001. *A Farm through Time.* Illustrated by Eric Thomas. New York and London: DK Publishers.

For younger children:
Gibbons, Gail. 1988. *Farming.* New York: Holiday House.

Directions for Participants

- Read one of the books on display by yourself, with a friend, or with a parent.
- Older children: Take one of the Barn concept web sheets.
- Keep track of the important ideas about farming for each time period on the sheet.
- Younger children: May color and create their barn from the barn pattern sheet.

Other Resources for This Center

Woods, Michael. 2000. *Ancient Agriculture: From Foraging to Farming.* Minneapolis: Runestone Press.

INTERACTIVE CENTER 2

INDUSTRIAL TECHNOLOGY

Three facets of this center can focus on the beginning and impact of the discovery of electricity, the development of simple machinery, and how trains as transportation allowed for more mobility between cities.

Electric Lightning

How Participants Can Interact

Ben Franklin's famous kite experiment started it all. The following two books are very readable and informative and can introduce both younger and older children to the concept of electricity.

Books on Display

Bang, Molly. 2004. *My Light.* New York: Blue Sky Press.
Schanzer, Rosalyn. 2003. *How Ben Franklin Stole the Lightning.* New York: HarperCollins.

In addition, an Internet station may be set up at the following address: http://www.pbs.org/benfranklin/shocking/index.html.

This is a wonderful interactive site that allows participants to experience static electricity, see Franklin's kite experiment, and how his lightning rod invention worked.

Make a Model of Franklin's Kite
Materials Needed

Nonbendable drinking straws
Thin twine
Cut pieces of ribbon strips
Construction paper
Scissors
Magic tape
Single hole punch
Template for kite, key, lightning bolt

Directions for Participants

1. Read *How Ben Franklin Stole the Lightning* by yourself, or with a friend or parent.
2. Take two drinking straws.
3. Make a t-shape and tie the straws together with the string by winding an **X** around both straws.

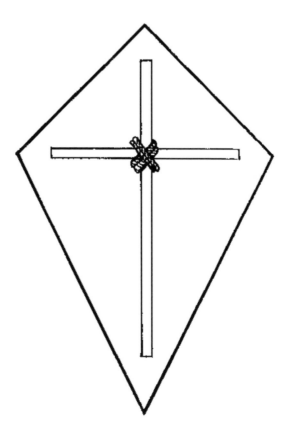

Kite with straws drawing.

Franklin's Kite Template

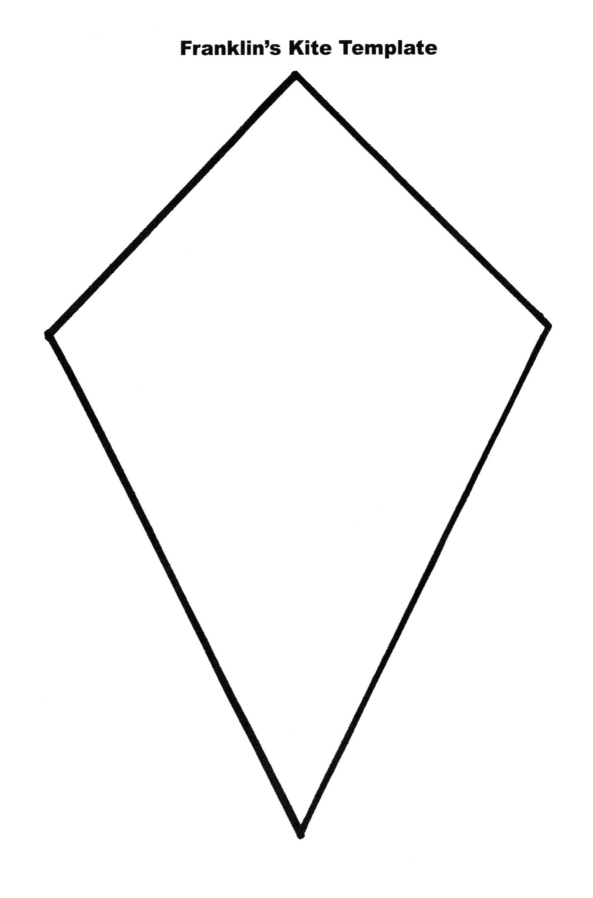

Franklin's Kite Templates

From *Summer Reading Renaissance: An Interactive Exhibits Approach* by Rita Soltan. Illustrations by Jill Reichenbach Fill. Westport, CT: Libraries Unlimited. Copyright © 2008.

4. Take a piece of construction paper and the kite template.
5. Trace around the template on the construction paper.
6. Cut the kite shape out.
7. Fold the kite lengthwise and open it.
8. Tape the straw t-shape to the center of the fold and across the top.
9. Punch a hole at the bottom of the kite.
10. Measure and cut some twine, about 12 inches long.
11. Tie the twine through the hole.
12. Take the key template and trace it on your extra piece of construction paper.
13. Cut your key out following the template diagram.
14. Thread the key through the bottom of your kite tail.
15. Measure and cut out another piece of twine, about 12 inches long.
16. Tie the twine to the bottom of the key as Ben Franklin did in the story.
17. You may add a couple of ribbons to the bottom of your kite tail.
18. Take the lightning bolt template and trace it on your unused paper.
19. Cut out your lightning bolt.
20. When you are finished, watch Ben Franklin's experiment on the Internet station provided.
21. Hang your kite and lightning bolt on the library display.

Additional Books on Electricity to Have on Display

Berger, Melvin. 2001. *Switch On, Switch Off.* Illustrated by Carolyn Croll. New York: Harper-Trophy.
Cole, Joanna, and Bruce Degen. 1997. *The Magic School Bus and the Electric Field Trip.* New York: Scholastic.
Godwin, Sam. 2002. *Which Switch is Which?* North Mankato, MN: Smart Apple Media.
Holderness, Jackie. 2002. *Why Does a Battery Make It Go?* Brookfield, CN: Copper Beech Books.
Llewellyn, Claire. 2005. *Electricity.* Photography by Ray Moller. Mankato, MN: Sea-to-Sea.
Nobleman, Marc Tyler. 2004. *The Light Bulb.* Mankato, MN: Capstone.
Pollard, Michael. 1995. *The Light Bulb and How It Changed the World.* New York: Facts on File.

Machines Make It Easy

One of the simplest machine concepts is that of the lever. Most children have been exposed to this concept through a seesaw. You may set up this center with the following books, video, and basic experiment.

Books on Display

Baker, Wendy, and Andrew Haslam. 1993. *Make It Work! Machines.* New York: Thomson Learning.
Dahl, Michael. 2006. *Scoop, Seesaw, and Raise: A Book about Levers.* Illustrated by Denise Shea. Minneapolis, MN: Picture Window Books.
Lampton, Christopher. 1991. *Seesaws, Nutcrackers, Brooms: Simple Machines That Are Really Levers.* Brookfield, CT: Millbrook Press.

Oxlade, Chris. 1998. *Machines.* Milwaukee, Gareth Stevens.

Royston, Angela. 2001. *Levers.* Chicago: Heineman Library.

Sadler, Wendy. 2005. *Machines Inside Machines: Using Levers.* Chicago: Raintree.

Tiner, John Hudson. 2003. *Levers.* North Mankato, MN: Smart Apple Media.

Tocci, Salvatore. 2003. *Experiments with Simple Machines.* New York: Children's Press.

Walker, Sally M., and Roseann Feldmann. 2000. *Levers.* Photographs by Andy King. Minneapolis, MN: Lerner.

Way Things Work: Levers. Wynnewood, PA: Schlessinger Media, 2003.

> Video: One of numerous in a wonderful series based on the book by David Macauley.

Welsbacher, Anne. 2001. *Levers.* Mankato, MN. Bridgestone Books.

Web Sites

The Inventor's Toolbox/Elements of Machines Web site from the Boston Museum of Science may be explored at an Internet station:

Boston Museum of Science. Inventors Toolbox.
http://www.mos.org/sln/Leonardo/InventorsToolbox.html.

How Participants Can Interact

By reading two stories that include the principle of a lever as demonstrated in a seesaw, children can then create their own version of a lever by following directions in the book *Levers* by Sally Walker and Roseann Feldmann, pages 16–23, listed above.

Materials Needed

12-inch wooden ruler
Crayon
Small unopened can of food
Some rubber bands

Young children may read one or both of the stories on display with a friend or parent.

Picture Book stories:

Albee, Sarah. 2003. *Clever Trevor.* Illustrated by Paige Billin-Frye. New York: Kane Press.

Tompert, Ann. 1993. *Just a Little Bit.* Illustrated by Lynn Munsinger. Boston: Houghton Mifflin.

Encourage readers to talk about what happened in either story and what needed to happen for the seesaw to move. By using the materials below, they can then demonstrate the concept presented in either or both stories.

Materials Needed

12-inch ruler
Wedge rubber eraser or small building block
Small unopened can of food

Directions for Participants

- Create a seesaw with the ruler and block or eraser as your fulcrum.
- Place the can on one side of the seesaw.
- What happens?
- What do you need to do to make the seesaw balance and then move down?

All Aboard—Trains, From Coal to Steam to Diesel

Trains are a much-loved interest for many children. A history and development of trains as transportation can be exhibited at this center. The development of the railroad not only allowed for better, faster transportation but it enabled trade and business to function at a larger capacity through the transporting of food and other materials and resources. You can be creative and have on hand a model train set or have children build and rebuild from a train-building kit. In addition, you may create your own train exhibit from a variety of cardboard boxes. A Web site with free instructions to help you do this can be found at:

http://mrmcgroovys.com/train.htm.

Books on Display

Fisher, Leonard Everett. 1979. *Nineteenth Century America: The Railroads*. New York: Holiday House.

———. 1992. *Tracks Across America: The Story of the American Railroad 1825–1900*. New York: Holiday House.

Fraser, Mary Ann. 1993. *Ten Mile Day and the Building of the Transcontinental Railroad*. New York: Henry Holt.

Meltzer, Milton. 2004. *Hear That Train Whistle Blow! How the Railroad Changed the World*. New York: Random House.

Morris, Neil. 2002. *Past and Present Trains*. North Mankato, MN: Smart Apple Media.

Simon, Seymour. 2002. *Seymour Simon's Book of Trains*. New York: HarperCollins.

Weitzman, David. 1999. *Locomotive: Building an Eight-Wheeler*. Boston: Houghton Mifflin.

Zimmerman, Karl. 2004. *Iron Locomotives: Whistling, Chugging, Smoking Iron Horses of the Past*. Honesdale, Penn: Boyds Mills Press.

Additional books for younger children:

Booth, Philip E. 2001. *Crossing*. Illustrations by Bagram Ibatoulline. Cambridge, MA: Candlewick.

Sturges, Philemon. 1999. *I Love Trains!* Illustrated by Shari Halpern. New York: HarperCollins.

How Participants Can Interact

Children can gain an understanding of the development of train engines and how trains had an impact on transportation and commerce. They can explore through the books on display or read a couple of specific titles together with a parent or friend.

A Gallery of Trains
Materials Needed

Books:

Emberley, Ed. 2002. *Ed Emberley's Drawing Book of Trucks and Trains.* Boston: Little, Brown.
Kuklin, Susan. 2003. *All Aboard! A True Train Story.* New York: Orchard Books.
London, Jonathan. 2007. *A Train Goes Clickety-Clack.* Illustrated by Denis Roche. New York: Henry Holt.
O'Brien, Patrick. 2000. *Steam, Smoke, and Steel: Back in Time with Trains.* Watertown, MA: Charlesbridge.

Drawing paper
Crayons, colored pencils, markers
Construction paper 9 x 12 for mounting
Various precut shapes of construction paper following templates below
Cotton balls
Glue sticks or glue

Directions for Participants

- **Older children** may read *Steam, Smoke, and Steel.*
- Use Ed Emberley's drawing book as a guide to draw versions of trains.
- Mount the drawings on the larger construction paper and hang around the room or in a designated train gallery space.
- **Younger children** may read together with a parent either *A Train Goes Clickety-Clack* or *All Aboard!*
- Younger children may create a construction paper train collage from various precut shapes mounted onto a larger piece of construction paper.
- Train collages may be hung in the gallery.

In addition, you can have younger children hear the various train sounds at an Internet station set to the following Web site:
Railway Station Productions
http://www.railwaystation.com/sounds1.html.

INTERACTIVE CENTER 3

COMMUNICATION

The way humans learned to communicate influenced how other forms of technology and innovative developments continued to evolve. Three activities illustrate a ladder of communication inventions through early writing, the first type of printing, and long-distance communication with the telegraph using Morse code.

Books on Display

Ganeri, Anita. 1997. *The Story of Communications.* New York: Oxford University Press.
Hamilton, Sue. 2000. *Communication: A Pictorial History of the Past One Thousand Years.* Edina, MN: Abdo.

Train Templates

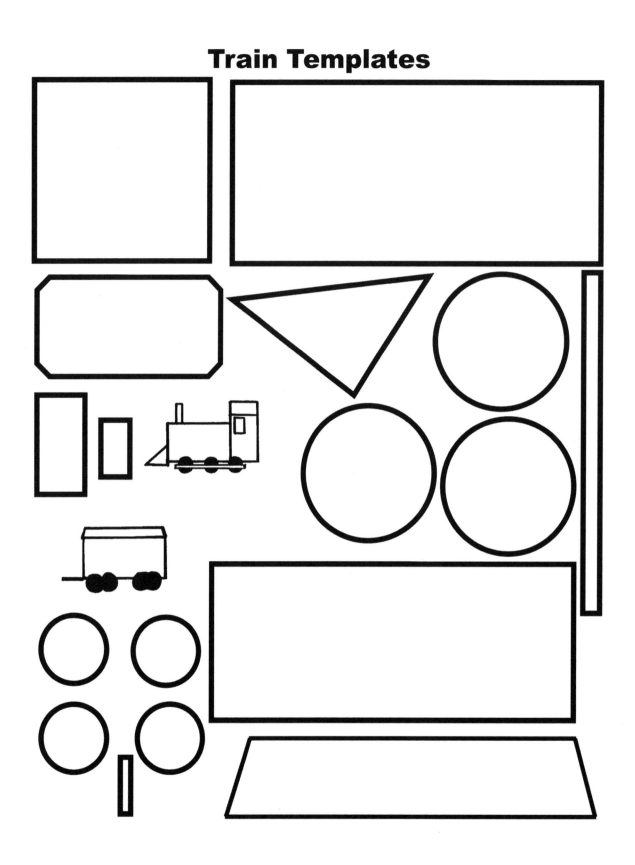

Hegedus, Alannah, and Kaitlin Rainey. 2001. *Bleeps and Blips to Rocket Ships: Great Inventions in Communications*. Toronto: Tundra Books.

Parker, Steve. 1998. *Communications Now and into the Future*. North Mankato, MN: Smart Apple Media.

Robb, Don. 2007. *Ox, House, Stick: The History of Our Alphabet*. Illustrated by Anne Smith. Watertown, MA: Charlesbridge.

Woods, Michael, and Mary B. Woods. 2000. *Ancient Communication: From Grunts to Graffiti*. Minneapolis: Runestone Press.

Early Writing—Hieroglyphics
How Participants Can Interact

Early Stone Age writing was in the form of paintings and engravings on cave walls. This eventually led to writings on clay tablets. A form of early writing is called hieroglyphics. Two of these writing systems, Egyptian and Mayan, can be explored in this activity.

Books on Display

Coulter, Laurie. 2001. *Secrets in Stone: All About Maya Hieroglyphs*. Illustrations by Sarah Jane English. Boston, MA: Little, Brown.

Donoughue, Carol. 1999. *The Mystery of the Hieroglyphs: The Story of the Rosetta Stone and the Race to Decipher Egyptian Hieroglyphs*. New York: Oxford University Press.

Fine, Jil. 2003. *Writing in Ancient Egypt*. New York: Rosen.

———. 2003. *Mayan Writing in Mesoamerica*. New York: Rosen.

Rossini, Stephane. 1989. *Egyptian Hieroglyphics: How to Read and Write Them*. New York: Dover.

Write Your Name in Egyptian Hieroglyphs
Materials Needed

Book:

Bower, Tamara. 2005. *How the Amazon Queen Fought the Prince of Egypt*. New York: Atheneum.

Reproducible Hieroglyphs sheet
Pencils or crayons
Sidewalk chalk

Directions for Participants

- Read the story *How the Amazon Queen Fought the Prince of Egypt* alone, or with a friend or parent.
- Notice how the story is also told in hieroglyphs.
- Try to reread the story from the hieroglyphs.
- Use the hieroglyphs alphabet sheet to create your name

On sunny warm summer days, this activity can move outside to a driveway, parking area, or sidewalk and children can use chalk to create their names.

Reading and Writing
Hieroglyphs

Early Egyptians wrote using picture letters called Hieroglyphs. There were over 700 of these letters, some of which stood for whole words. Word signs were simple pictures illustrating an object or action.

For example, a series of wavy lines was drawn to mean water.

Other symbols stood for one or two letters or sounds.

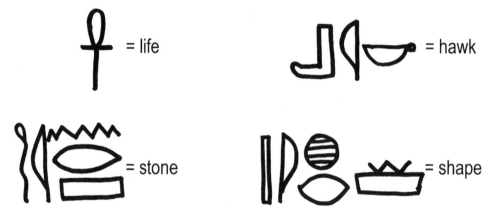

Gradually hieroglyphs became less detailed to make them quicker and easier to write. Scribes wrote with these to record everyday documents such as tax records.

Hieroglyphs

A	B	C	D	E	F
G	H	I	J	K	L
M	N	O	P	Q	R
S	T	U	V	W	X
Y	Z				

Use the hieroglyph sounds above to write your name. While Ancient Egyptians did not have signs for all of the vowel sounds, all the vowels are listed in this chart to help you write your name and story more easily.

Your name:

From *Summer Reading Renaissance: An Interactive Exhibits Approach* by Rita Soltan. Illustrations by Jill Reichenbach Fill. Westport, CT: Libraries Unlimited. Copyright © 2008.

Create a Mayan Message
Materials Needed

Books:

Coulter, Laurie. 2001. *Secrets in Stone: All About Maya Hieroglyphs.* Illustrations by Sarah Jane
    English. Boston, MA: Little, Brown.
Wisniewski, David. 1991. *Rain Player.* New York: Clarion.

Copy paper
Colored pencils

Directions for Participants

- Read the story *Rain Player* by yourself, with a parent, or with a friend. At the
  beginning of the story, the priest, or *Ah Kin Mai,* uses his charts and calendar
  to predict the weather.
- In the book *Secrets in Stone: All About Maya Hieroglyphs,* pay attention to the
  various charts, calendars, and hieroglyphs throughout the book, especially
  pages 12–13.
- Use the "Glyphmaster" at the back of the book to create your own Mayan
  codex (a book with the Mayan symbols). The last page of *Secrets in Stone* offers
  a raised symbol chart for the Mayan hieroglyphs with directions on how to
  make a rubbing from the symbols.
- Take a piece of copy paper and fold it into 4 accordion folds, so you have 4
  columns.

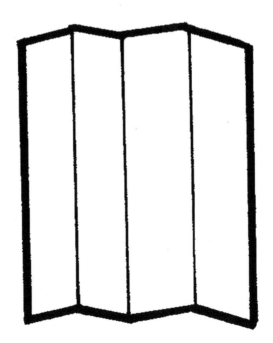

Accordion fold.

- Use the pencils to make a rubbing of the symbols.

Drawing/Rubbing.

- You may use the symbols to create your name or a secret message.

Reading for Everyone—Printing

The invention of the printing press and the printing of the Gutenberg Bible in 1456 revolutionized the education of all people as opposed to the privileged few.

Books on Display

Fisher, Leonard Everett. 1993. *Gutenberg.* New York: Macmillan.

Koscielniak, Bruce. 2003. *Johann Gutenberg and the Amazing Printing Press.* Boston: Houghton Mifflin.

Krensky, Stephen. 1996. *Breaking into Print: Before and After the Invention of the Printing Press.* Illustrated by Bonnie Christensen. Boston: Little, Brown.

How Participants Can Interact

Reading any or all of the three books can acquaint participants with the development of writing, scribing, and the invention of printing. They may then create versions of their own printing modeled after the printing craft books below. For a visual representation of early printing and digital facsimiles of the original Gutenberg Bible, set up an Internet station at the following Web site from the British Library:
http://www.bl.uk/treasures/gutenberg/homepage.html.

Materials Needed

Choice of materials can be determined from a variety of easy-to-reproduce and create printing projects from three craft books:

O'Reilly, Susie. 1993. *Block Printing.* New York: Thomson Learning.
Includes easy instructions on creating stamp pads with plastic containers, paints, and foam sponges (page 16).

Oxlade, Chris. 2005. *Writing and Printing.* North Mankato, MN: Sea-to-Sea.
Pages 20–21 offer an easy way to create block letter printing.

Stocks, Sue. 1994. *Printing.* New York: Thomson Learning.
A variety of suggestions including "relief printing with string" pages 22–23.

Can We Talk?—The Telegraph, the Telephone, and IM (instant messaging)

Children today are more than aware of communicating by telephone and instant messaging. This center can focus on the forerunner with the invention of the telegraph and Morse code.

Books on Display

Alphin, Elaine Marie. 2001. *Telephones.* Minneapolis: Carolrhoda.

Alter, Judy. 2003. *Samuel F. B. Morse: Inventor and Code Creator.* Chanhassen, MN: Child's World.

Cefrey, Holly. 2003. *The Inventions of Alexander Graham Bell: The Telephone.* New York: Rosen.

Kerby, Mona. 1991. *Samuel Morse.* New York: Franklin Watts.

Linder, Greg. 1999. *Alexander Graham Bell: A Photo-Illustrated Biography.* Mankato, MN: Bridgestone.

Matthews, Tom L. 1999. *Always Inventing: A Photobiography of Alexander Graham Bell.* Washington, DC: National Geographic Society.

McCormick, Anita Louise. 2004. *The Invention of the Telegraph and Telephone in American History.* Berkeley Heights, NJ: Enslow Publishers.

Micklos, John. 2006. *Alexander Graham Bell Inventor of the Telephone.* New York: HarperCollins.

Nobleman, Marc Tyler. 2004. *The Telephone.* North Mankato, MN: Capstone Press.

Sherrow, Victoria. 2001. *Alexander Graham Bell.* Illustrated by Elaine Verstraete. Minneapolis: Carolrhoda.

Web Sites

The Smithsonian Web site offers a page on inventors with two exhibits for the early telegraph:

http://www.150.si.edu/150trav/remember/amerinv.htm.

How Participants Can Interact

Focusing on the telegraph and Morse code, participants can read two stories and then write and send a telegraphic message.

Materials Needed

Books:

Barasch, Lynne. 2000. *Radio Rescue.* New York: Farrar, Straus, and Giroux.

Quackenbush, Robert. 1983. *Quick, Annie, Give Me a Catchy Line!: A Story of Samuel F. B. Morse.* Englewood Cliffs, NJ.

Simple Telegraph Machine

You may create a couple of simple telegraph machines for this center and have them available for participants to use. Instructions for making a simple telegraph machine can be found at:

Yes Mag: The Science Magazine for Adventurous Minds. Peter Piper Publishing, Inc.
http://www.yesmag.bc.ca/projects/telegraph.html.

Morse Code

· — **A**	— · · · **B**	— · — · **C**	— · · **D**	· **E**	· · — · **F**
— — · **G**	· · · · **H**	· · **I**	· — — — **J**	— · — **K**	· — · · **L**
— — **M**	— · **N**	— — — **O**	· — — · **P**	— — · — **Q**	· — · **R**
· · · **S**	— **T**	· · — **U**	· · · — **V**	· — — **W**	— · · — **X**
— · — — **Y**	— — · · **Z**				

Your telegraphic message:

From *Summer Reading Renaissance: An Interactive Exhibits Approach* by Rita Soltan. Illustrations by Jill Reichenbach Fill. Westport, CT: Libraries Unlimited. Copyright © 2008.

Morse code worksheet
Pencils
Flashlight

Directions for Participants

- Read *Quick, Annie, Give Me a Catchy Line!* by yourself, with a friend, or with a parent.
- Take a worksheet and write out a message in Morse code.
- Send your message using the telegraph machine.
- See if your partner can understand the message you sent.
- Read *Radio Rescue* alone, with a friend, or with a parent.
- Take a worksheet and write out a message in Morse code.
- Use the flashlight to send your message to your partner just as the boy in the story sends his message to the sailors anchored in the Hudson River.
- See if your partner can understand the message you sent.

Ham radio.

Radio Rescue introduces the reader to communication through ham radios. For information on how this is still being done today with ham radio clubs around the country, visit the Web site:
The American Radio Relay League
http://www.hello-radio.org/.
You can find a local club to help develop a program or even set up a ham radio display at your center. You may also set up an Internet station bookmarked at this site for participants to explore the history and how ham radio is still a hobby in today's world of modern communications.

Unit 3 The Inventor's Hall of Fame

The great inventors, their lives and innovative ideas, are the bulk of this unit. Biographies and the stories behind the most influential or groundbreaking inventions can be your focus. A rotating display of books together with exhibit material you can either purchase from an educational vendor or create yourself can keep your biography section circulating. To help you sort through the decades and centuries in order to choose key inventors, begin with some collected biographies such as:

Clements, Gillian. 1996. *The Picture History of Great Inventors.* New York: Knopf.
Discovery Communications. 2002. *Inventors & Inventions.* Interactive Media CD-ROM. Bethesda, MD: Discovery Communications.
Hudson, Wade. 2003. *Book of Black Heroes: Scientists, Healers, and Inventors.* East Orange, NJ: Just Us Books.
Sandler, Martin W. 1995. *Inventors: A Library of Congress Book.* New York: HarperCollins.
Thimmesh, Catherine. 2000. *Girls Think of Everything: Stories of Ingenious Inventions by Women.* Boston: Houghton Mifflin.
Williams, Marcia. 2005. *Hooray for Inventors!* Cambridge, MA: Candlewick.

You may also begin by working from the following list of inventors. Titles are all biographies, except when noted. You may wish to have a simple craft or activity for each at the display table, such as a simple telescope for Galileo. The following four figures are a sampling of how you may develop your rotating display.

Galileo

Boerst, William J. 2004. *Galileo Galilei and the Science of Motion.* Greensboro, NC: Morgan Reynolds.
Fisher, Leonard Everett. 1992. *Galileo.* New York: Macmillan.
Lewis, J. Patrick. 2005. *Galileo's Universe, Poems.* Illustrated by Tom Curry. Paper engineering by Bruce Foster. Mankato, MN: Creative Editions.
   Narrative poetry about the life and achievements of this great astronomer.
O'Donnell, Kerri. 2003. *Galileo: Man of Science.* New York: Rosen.
Panchyk, Richard. 2005. *Galileo for Kids: His Life and Ideas, 25 Activities.* Chicago: Chicago Review Press.
Sis, Peter. 1996. *Starry Messenger.* New York: Farrar, Straus, & Giroux.

Interactive Telescope Activity/Experiment

While Galileo did not invent the telescope, he did create a three-powered spyglass that allowed him to view the Moon for the first time. More information is available at the following Web site:
   The Galileo Project
   http://galileo.rice.edu/sci/instruments/telescope.html.

Resource Books

Bullock, Linda. 2003. *Looking through a Telescope.* New York: Children's Press.
Carson, Mary Kay. 2006. *Exploring the Solar System: A History with 22 Activities.* Chicago: Chicago Review Press.
Orr, Tamra. 2004. *The Telescope.* New York: Franklin Watts.
Simon, Seymour. 2002. *Destination Space.* New York: HarperCollins.
   Denotes new discoveries with the Hubble Telescope.

Telescope.

Web Sites

An easy-to-reproduce telescope experiment with two magnifying lenses can be obtained at the following Web site:

Discovery Education

http://school.discovery.com/sciencefaircentral/jvc/surpscifacts/telescope.html.

Leonardo da Vinci

Anderson, Maxine. 2006. *Amazing Leonardo da Vinci Inventions You Can Build Yourself.* White River Junction, VT: Nomad Press.

Anholt, Laurence. 2000. *Leonardo and the Flying Boy: A Story About Leonardo da Vinci.* Hauppauge, New York: Barron's.

Byrd, Robert. 2003. *Leonardo Beautiful Dreamer.* New York: Dutton.

Herbert, Janis. 1998. *Leonardo da Vinci for Kids: His Life and Ideas, 21 Activities.* Chicago: Chicago Review.

Krull, Kathleen. 2005. *Leonardo da Vinci.* Illustrated by Boris Kulikov. New York: Viking.

McDonald, Fiona. 2001. *The World in the Time of Leonardo da Vinci.* Philadelphia: Chelsea.

O'Connor, Barbara. 2003. *Leonardo da Vinci: Renaissance Genius.* Minneapolis: Carolrhoda.
Visconti, Guido. 2000. *The Genius of Leonardo.* Illustrated by Bimba Landmann. New York: Barefoot Books.

Interactive Activity—Leonardo's Parachute

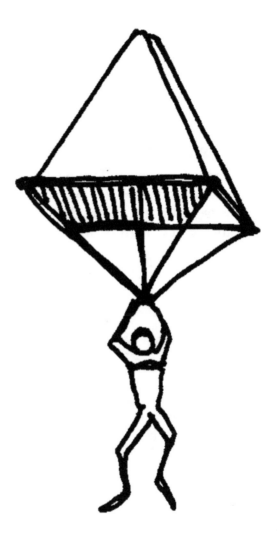

Leonardo's Parachute.

Leonardo da Vinci was convinced that a flying machine would and could someday be created to allow man to fly.

How Participants Can Interact

Children can read *Leonardo and the Flying Boy: A Story About Leonardo da Vinci,* a short, illustrated fictional version of a Leonardo flying invention, and then recreate a parachute from the book *Amazing Leonardo da Vinci Inventions You Can Build Yourself,* pages 88–91. You may also choose another activity from this book if you wish. Set up your center area with materials and directions as outlined by the author.

Thomas Edison

Adler, David A. 1990. *Thomas Alva Edison Great Inventor.* Illustrated by Lyle Miller. New York: Holiday House.

———. 1996. *A Picture Book of Thomas Alva Edison.* Illustrated by John and Alexandra Wallner. New York: Holiday House.

Carlson, Laurie. 2006. *Thomas Edison for Kids: His Life and Ideas, 21 Activities.* Chicago: Chicago Review Press.

Dooling, Michael. 2005. *Young Thomas Edison.* New York: Holiday House.

Fandel, Jennifer. 2005. *The Light Bulb.* Mankato, MN: Creative Education.

Gomez, Rebecca. 2003. *Thomas Edison.* Edina, MN: Abdo Publishing.

Linder, Greg. 1999. *Thomas Edison: A Photo-Illustrated Biography.* Mankato, MN: Bridgestone.

Parker, Steve. 1992. *Thomas Edison and Electricity.* New York: HarperCollins.

How Participants Can Interact

An Internet station may be set for the following Library of Congress Web site, where a wealth of information is available. Downloading the six-part movie *A Day with Thomas Edison* (1922) places kids and participants directly into the inventor's world. This can be accessed at the Library of Congress: Inventing Entertainment The Edison Companies Web site:

http://memory.loc.gov/ammem/ndlpedu/collections/ed/file.html.

Wilbur and Orville Wright

Carson, Mary Kay. 2003. *The Wright Brothers for Kids: How They Invented the Airplane, 21 Activities Exploring the Science and History of Flight.* Illustrated by Laura D'Argo. Chicago: Chicago Review Press.

Collins, Mary. 2003. *Airborne: A Photobiography of Wilbur and Orville Wright.* Washington DC: National Geographic, 2003.

Edwards, Pamela Duncan. 2003. *The Wright Brothers.* Illustrated by Henry Cole. New York: Hyperion.

Hill, Lee Sullivan. 2006. *The Flyer Flew! The Invention of the Airplane.* Illustrated by Craig Orback. Minneapolis: Millbrook Press.

McPherson, Stephanie Sammartino. 2004. *Wilbur & Orville Wright: Taking Flight.* Minneapolis: Carolrhoda.

Tieck, Sarah. 2007. *The Wright Brothers.* Edina, MN: Abdo.

Wadsworth, Ginger. 2004. *The Wright Brothers.* Minneapolis: Lerner.

Wyborny, Sheila. 2004. *The Wright Brothers.* San Diego: Kidhaven Press.

How Participants Can Interact

A fictitious version of the Wright Brothers' introduction to flying machines can be read and followed by a paper-flying project or activity. A good book option is:

Glass, Andrew. 2003. *The Wondrous Whirligig: The Wright Brothers' First Flying Machine.* New York: Holiday House.

Two books to help you develop an origami paper-flying project are:

LaFosse, Michael G. 2004. *Making Origami Paper Airplanes Step by Step.* New York: Power Kids Press.

Temko, Florence. 1996. *Paper Magic: Planes and Other Flying Things.* Brookfield, CT: Millbrook.

The Invention Convention Memory Game

This activity can be developed to include information about odd and unusual inventions and their inventors. Use the cards on the reproducible pages to create a laminated set of memory game cards.

Resources for This Activity

Borden, Louise. 2003. *Sea Clocks: The Story of Longitude.* Illustrated by Erik Blegvad. New York: Margaret McElderry.

Carlson, Laurie. 2003. *Queen of Inventions: How the Sewing Machine Changed the World.* Brookfield, CT: Millbrook.

Foltz, Charlotte. 1991. *Mistakes That Worked.* Illustrated by John O'Brien. New York: Doubleday.

Fradin, Dennis. 2006. *With A Little Luck: Surprising Stories of Amazing Discoveries.* New York: Dutton.

Greenstein, Elaine. 2003. *Ice Cream Cones for Sale!* New York: Scholastic.

Harper, Charise Mericle. 2001. *Imaginative Inventions: The Who, What, Where, When, and Why of Roller Skates, Potato Chips, Marbles, and Pie.* Boston: Little, Brown.

Lasky, Kathryn. 2003. *The Man Who Made Time Travel.* Illustrated by Kevin Hawkes. New York: Farrar, Straus, and Giroux.

McCully, Emily Arnold. 2006. *Marvelous Mattie: How Margaret E. Knight Became an Inventor.* New York: Farrar, Straus and Giroux.

Murphy, Jim. 1978. *Weird and Wacky Inventions.* New York: Crown.
    While this is old, it includes some great drawings with clues to guess what they are for.

Murphy, Patricia J. 2004. *Grace Hopper Computer Whiz.* Berkley Heights, NJ: Enslow.

Thimmesh, Catherine. 2000. *Girls Think of Everything: Stories of Ingenious Inventions by Women.* Boston: Houghton Mifflin.

Williams, Marcia. 2005. *Hooray for Inventors!* Cambridge, MA: Candlewick.

Wulffson, Don. 1997. *The Kid Who Invented the Popsicle: And Other Surprising Stories about Inventions.* New York: Dutton.

———. 2000. *Toys! Amazing Stories Behind Some Great Inventions.* Illustrations by Laurie Keller. New York: Henry Holt.

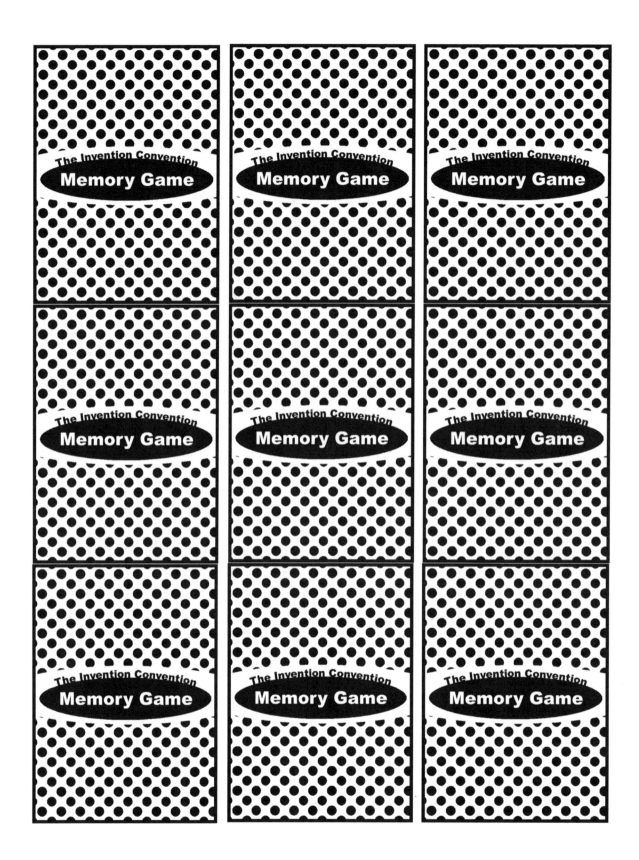

From *Summer Reading Renaissance: An Interactive Exhibits Approach* by Rita Soltan. Illustrations by Jill Reichenbach Fill. Westport, CT: Libraries Unlimited. Copyright © 2008.

**Guglielmo Marconi,
The Radio**

**Guglielmo Marconi,
The Radio**

**Thomas Edison,
The Phonograph**

**Thomas Edison,
The Phonograph**

**George de Mestral,
Velcro**

**George de Mestral,
Velcro**

**Ladislao Biro,
Ballpoint Pen**

**Ladislao Biro,
Ballpoint Pen**

**Tim Berners-Lee,
World Wide Web with
his program "Enquire
Within"**

**Doug Engelbart,
Computer Mouse**

**Doug Engelbart,
Computer Mouse**

**Randolph Smith
and
Kenneth House,
Smoke Alarm**

**Randolph Smith
and
Kenneth House,
Smoke Alarm**

**Antonio Meucci,
Developed the idea
for the telephone
by carrying the
human voice
through wires**

**Antonio Meucci,
Developed the idea
for the telephone
by carrying the
human voice
through wires**

**Alexander
Graham Bell,
The Telephone**

**Alexander
Graham Bell,
The Telephone**

From *Summer Reading Renaissance: An Interactive Exhibits Approach* by Rita Soltan. Illustrations by Jill Reichenbach Fill. Westport, CT: Libraries Unlimited. Copyright © 2008.

**Steve Jobs
and
Stephen Wozniak,
Personal Computer**

**Steve Jobs
and
Stephen Wozniak,
Personal Computer**

**Karl Benz,
Motorcar**

**Karl Benz,
Motorcar**

**Gideon Sundback,
Zipper**

**Gideon Sundback,
Zipper**

**Rowland Hill,
Postage Stamp**

**Rowland Hill,
Postage Stamp**

**Tim Berners-Lee,
World Wide Web with
his program "Enquire
Within"**

**Isaac Singer,
Sewing Machine**

**Walter
Frederick Morrison,
Frisbee Flying Disc**

**Walter
Frederick Morrison,
Frisbee Flying Disc**

**Silvano Armato,
Eye Glasses**

**Silvano Armato,
Eye Glasses**

**Chuko Liang,
Wheelbarrows**

**Chuko Liang,
Wheelbarrows**

**Hubert Cecil Booth,
Vacuum Cleaner**

**Hubert Cecil Booth,
Vacuum Cleaner**

**Italo Marchiony,
Ice Cream Cone**

**Italo Marchiony,
Ice Cream Cone**

**Grace Hopper,
Computer Compiler**

**Margaret E. Knight,
"The Lady Edison,"
Invented the machine
that cuts and glues
together
a flat-bottomed
paper bag.**

**Margaret E. Knight,
"The Lady Edison,"
Invented the machine
that cuts and glues
together
a flat-bottomed
paper bag.**

**Grace Hopper,
Computer Compiler**

**John Harrison,
Seafaring Clock
Navigation Chronometer**

**John Harrison,
Seafaring Clock
Navigation Chronometer**

**Isaac Singer,
Sewing Machine**

Unit 4 Be Your Own Inventor

Plan this unit for the end of the summer. However, you should encourage participants to create and invent all summer long and bring their innovations to a weeklong invention convention exhibit. Whether you open your community room or work within your youth room, a display and even a day or evening invention fair can allow young inventors to demonstrate their ideas for your open house closing summer program event.

Resources to Keep on Hand through the Summer

Casey, Susan. 2005. *Kids Inventing! A Handbook for Young Inventors.* Hoboken, NJ: John Wiley & Sons.
Erlbach, Arlene. 1997. *The Kid's Invention Book.* Minneapolis: Lerner.
St. George, Judith. 2002. *So You Want to Be an Inventor?* Illustrated by David Small. New York: Philomel Books.

Web Sites

By Kids For Kids. http://www.bkfk.com/index.asp.
    This is an informative site to help kids bring their ideas to fruition that offers help on the process of inventing, patents, marketing, etc., at no charge to children, parents, or teachers.
United States Patent and Trademark Office. Kids' Page. http://www.uspto.gov/go/kids/index.html.
Young Inventors International. http://www.younginventorsinternational.com/index.php.

Add Pizzazz to Invention Convention

During portions of the two-week unit periods, event programming can be planned to include any of the following ideas:

Mancala Game Night

Hold an official mancala evening. The popularity of this African-based game can allow families to bring in their personal wooden sets or include a segment in the program where everyone makes a set from egg cartons and beans.

Model Train Display

Solicit help from a local model train club or enthusiast to develop a working display for your railroad unit. Check out the following Web sites for help in locating a club in your area:
    The Internet Train Club
    http://www.trainclub.com/.
    Rails USA Rail Site Directory
    http://www.railsusa.com/links/Model_Railroad_Clubs/.

Wacky Inventions and the Cartoonist

Create a display commemorating Rube Goldberg, the cartoonist and engineer who devised complicated contraptions to accomplish simple tasks. Check out the following Web site for ideas and help with this program idea:

http://www.rubegoldberg.com/

Hire a local cartoonist to provide a how-to drawing hour for your young patrons' wacky ideas and solutions.

Night of Intrigue and Secret Communications

Hold a charades-style team game night with challenges that must be interpreted from Morse code and Egyptian and Mayan Hieroglyphs.

Annotated Bibliography of Related Fiction for Invention Convention

Appleton, Victor. 2006. *Tom Swift Young Inventor series.* New York: Aladdin Paperbacks. Grades 3–5.

   Newly redone editions of the 1930's science fiction series. Titles include: *The Robot Olympics, Into the Abyss, Rocket Racers, On Top of the World, The Space Hotel.*

Asch, Frank. 2006. *Star Jumper: Journal of a Cardboard Genius.* Toronto, Kids Can Press. Grades 2–4.

———. 2007. *Gravity Buster: Journal #2 of a Cardboard Genius.*

   Alex, the inventor of a cardboard spaceship, attempts to travel to a little brother–free planet. Easy chapter book includes copious drawings of Alex's inventions.

Baker, Keith. 2006. *On the Go With Mr. and Mrs. Green.* New York: Harcourt. Grades K–2.

   The loving alligator couple returns in this beginning-to-read series to invent a couple of wacky and useful inventions—a slicing machine and a sun scooter.

Benton, Jim. 2004. *Attack of the 50-Foot Cupid.* New York: Aladdin. Grades 1–3.

   Young Franny K. Stein, mad scientist and inventor, has to rectify her Valentine Poem generator when her new lab assistant and pet dog Igor accidentally sets it loose with a 50-foot cupid. Lots of laughs with this early chapter choice.

Bernasconi, Pablo. 2005. *Captain Arsenio: Inventions and (Mis)Adventures in Flight.* Boston: Houghton Mifflin. Grades 4–6.

   The exploits of an imaginary eighteenth-century aviator are documented with diagrams and illustrations of failed attempts in this invented flight diary, filled with some slapstick humor.

Carlson, Drew. 2007. *Attack of the Turtle.* Illustrated by David A. Johnson. Grand Rapids, MI: Eerdsmans. Grades 5–7.

   During the Revolutionary War, 14-year-old Nate, a patriot too young to fight, joins his inventor cousin David Bushnell to build a water machine that can explode bombs under water. An adventurous historical fiction novel based on true events of the invention of the first submarine built to engage in warfare against the British navy.

   Another related book of interest is:

   Lefkowitz, Arthur. 2006. *Bushnell's Submarine.* New York: Scholastic.

   A nonfiction account of the building and use of the "American Turtle."

Dodds, Dayle Ann. 2004. *Henry's Amazing Machine.* Pictures by Kyrsten Brooker. New York: Farrar, Straus and Giroux. Grades K–3.

   Henry builds and builds an incredible machine that takes over every inch of his home and town until he finds a real purpose for its use.

Drummond, Allan. 2003. *The Flyers.* New York: Farrar, Straus and Giroux. Grades 2–4.

   In 1903, a group of children on the beach at Kitty Hawk, North Carolina, dream of flying and witness the first flight of the Wright brothers.

Geisert, Arthur. 2005. *Lights Out.* Boston: Houghton Mifflin. Grades 2–5.
   When a small pig is reluctant to turn off the light at bedtime because he wants to avoid the scary darkness of his room, he creates a complicated and convoluted contraption that moves through a series of mechanical devices in order to arrive at the light switch after he is asleep. A wordless story filled with detailed paintings perfect for young writers and enthusiastic dreamers.

Greenburg, J. C. 2002–2006. *The Andrew Lost series.* New York: Random House. Grades 2–4.
   Ten-year-old Andrew invents a shrinking machine and gets sucked into it with his cousin Judy, where they are reduced to microscopic size and get lost in a variety of places.

Haseley, Dennis. 2002. *The Amazing Thinking Machine.* New York: Dial. Grades 4–5.
   During the Depression, eight-year-old Patrick and his brother Roy build an answer machine out of an old typewriter and spare parts to raise money from the neighborhood kids and help their mother make ends meet while their unemployed father has left town to look for work.

Lasky, Kathryn. 2004. *Humphrey, Albert, and the Flying Machine.* Illustrated by John Manders. New York: Harcourt. Grades 3–5.
   In a spoof of the traditional Sleeping Beauty fairy tale, the princess's brothers awake a bit earlier following the hundred-year period and go in search of a suitable candidate to break the spell; encounter the inventor/scientist David Bernoulli, who developed the principle that allows airplane wings to lift and therefore fly.

MacGill-Callahan, Sheila. 1997. *To Capture the Wind.* Paintings by Gregory Manchess. New York: Dial Books. Grades 3–5.
   A legendary folk story of how a young maiden solves four riddles to free her lover from kidnapping pirates and invents the sails of a ship.

Montgomery, Claire and Monte. 2005. *Hubert Invents the Wheel.* Illustrated by Jeff Shelly. New York: Walker. Grades 4–6.
   A satirical, comedic look at how Hubert's invention leads to future complications such as traffic jams and war machines.

Ogren, Cathy Stefanec. 2002. *Adventures of Archie Featherspoon.* Illustrated by Jack E. Davis. New York: Aladdin. Grades K–2.
   A Wild West tall tale in which Archie the inventor uses his clever inventions to outwit the outlaws when they come riding into town on the heels of the latest twister. Beginning-to-read fun.

Pelley, Kathleen T. 2006. *Inventor McGregor.* Illustrated by Michael Chesworth. New York: Farrar Straus Giroux. Grades K–2.
   When the highly successful Inventor McGregor is asked to come and work for the Royal Society of Inventors, away from familiar surroundings, he loses his inspiration and cannot focus on any more inventions.

Perry, Andrea. 2003. *Here's What You Do When You Can't Find Your Shoe: Ingenious Inventions for Pesky Problems.* Illustrated by Alan Snow. New York: Atheneum. Grades K–4.
   A series of short poems describing offbeat inventions like footsie floss, hotels for bugs, and a super spider spotter for Miss Muffet.

Scieszka, Jon. 2004. *Da Wild Da Crazy Da Vinci.* Illustrated by Adam McCauley. New York: Viking. Grades 3–5.
   In this Time Warp Trio edition, Fred, Joe, and Sam land in sixteenth-century Italy, meet Leonardo da Vinci, and discover the inventions of the time, including that of Thomas Crapper, the inventor of the toilet.

Sidman, Joyce. 2002. *Eureka! Poems About Inventors.* Illustrated by K. Bennett Chavez. Brook-
    field, CT: Millbrook. Grades 4–7.
    A collection of free verse illustrating inventors through time, from "Wizard" for Leonardo
    da Vinci and "Ode to Spode" for the invention of the dishwasher to "Enquire Within" for
    the invention of the World Wide Web.

9

Traverse the Universe

Outline of Program

Weeks 1 & 2—Mysteries of the Universe
1. Big Bang
2. Milky Way
3. Astronomical discoveries

Weeks 3 & 4—Planetarium
1. Solar system
2. Comets, asteroids, meteorites
3. Pluto

Weeks 5 & 6—Skylore
1. Constellations
2. Planet names
3. Writing

Weeks 7 & 8—Exploration
1. Trivia
2. Space Station
3. Extraterrestrials

The mysteries of the universe, from its beginnings with the "Big Bang" theory to its expansive unknown, have intrigued humanity for thousands of years. Similarly, the planets and outer space have been a favorite library summer reading theme. This program takes the traditional theme one step further with exhibits and interactive centers that include reading, writing, and some creative ways of exploring the wonders of the vast cosmos.

Unit 1 The Mysteries of the Universe

Establish your summer theme with this unit offering a bit of history into some of the theories of the origin of the universe, the science of astronomy, and how, over the centuries, ideas concerning the development of the solar system and its galaxy known as the Milky Way evolved.

Resources for This Unit

Banquieri, Eduardo. 2006. *Space.* Translated by Patrick Clark. Illustrations by Marcel Socias Studio. Philadelphia: Chelsea House.

Carson, Mary Kay. 2006. *Exploring the Solar System: A History with 22 Activities.* Chicago: Chicago Review Press.

Claybourne, Anna. 2006. *The Solar System.* New York: Chelsea House.

Fleisher, Paul. 2006. *The Big Bang.* Minneapolis, MN: Twenty-First Century Books.

Furniss, Tim. 2002. *The Atlas of Space Exploration.* New York: Michael Friedman Publishing Group.

Gifford, Clive. 2001. *The Kingfisher Facts and Records Book of Space.* New York: Kingfisher.

Hill, Maureen. 1998. *Stars and Planets: The Mystery of Outer Space, Explained in Glorious Colour.* London, Caxton Editions.

Jackson, Ellen B. 2002. *Looking for Life in the Universe: The Search for Extraterrestrial Intelligence.* Photographs by Nic Bishop. Boston: Houghton Mifflin.

Jefferis, David. 2006. *Black Holes and Other Bizarre Space Objects.* New York: Crabtree.

Kupperberg, Paul. 2005. *Hubble and the Big Bang.* New York: Rosen Group.

Morgan, Jennifer. 2002. *Born with a Bang: The Universe Tells Our Cosmic Story.* Book 1. Nevada City, CA: Dawn Publications.

Rau, Dana Meachen. 2005. *The Milky Way and Other Galaxies.* Minneapolis, MN: Compass Point Books.

Simon, Seymour. 2002. *Destination Space.* New York: HarperCollins.

———. *The Universe.* New York: Morrow Junior Books, 1998.

World Book. 2006. *Galaxies and the Universe.* Chicago: World Book.

Two activity books to help you create interactive centers:

Love, Ann, and Jane Drake. 2004. *The Kid's Book of the Night Sky.* Illustrated by Heather Collins. Toronto: Kids Can Press.

Nicolson, Cynthia Pratt, and Paulette Bourgeois. 2007. *The Jumbo Book of Space.* Illustrated by Bill Slavin. Toronto, Kids Can Press.

Web Sites

NASA Solar System for Kids. http://sse.jpl.nasa.gov/kids/index.cfm.
    Get started with ideas presented in this well-designed and detailed site that presents everything from interactive activities to paper plate innovations for you to implement.

NASA. StarChild: A Learning Center for Young Astronomers.
    http://starchild.gsfc.nasa.gov/docs/StarChild/StarChild.html.

New York Public Library On-Lion for Kids. Space and Space Travel.
    http://kids.nypl.org/science/space.cfm.
    Provides a well-researched list of good links to educational Web sites.

Windows to the Universe.

University Corporation for Atmospheric Research at the University of Michigan
    http://www.windows.ucar.edu/windows.html
    Includes a teacher's resource link and numerous ideas and interactive games.

Ask a librarian to stamp your game sheet with a star for every box you complete.

Attend a Program	Read for One Hour	Read about an Astronaut or Astronomer	Read for One Hour	Attend a Program
Read for 1/2 Hour	Poetry Potpourri (Read a Book of Poems)	Finish a Cosmic Interactive Center	Find the Dewey Number for Books on the Solar System	Read for 1/2 Hour
Read for One Hour	Find the Dewey Number for Space Travel	Attend the Open House Kickoff	Read a Fairytale or a Picture Book	Read for One Hour
Read for 1/2 Hour	Finish a Cosmic Interactive Center	Read a Short Story	Finish a Cosmic Interactive Center	Read for 1/2 Hour
Attend a Program	Read for One Hour	Finish a Cosmic Interactive Center	Read for One Hour	Attend a Program

5 Boxes Stamped = Your Name on the Space Shuttle
10 Boxes Stamped = Your Name on the International Space Station
15 Boxes Stamped = Your Name on a Cosmic Certificate

Traverse the Universe

Summer Reading Program

★ Register.

★ Read-to-Me to Grade 8 may participate.

★ Take your reading game sheet home and READ, READ, READ! Keep track of the time you spend reading.

★ Participate in our interactive centers and attend library programs!

★ When you've completed a box on your game sheet, ask a librarian to stamp the appropriate box.

★ Complete 5 boxes — put your name on the Space Shuttle.

★ Complete 10 boxes — put your name on the International Space Station.

★ Complete 15 boxes — receive a Cosmic Certificate, Books, or a coupon.

★ Complete all boxes — receive an entry in the Grand Prize Drawing!

★ The LAST DAY to have game sheets stamped is _____.

★ Enter the weekly lotto each time you visit the library (one entry per day) for a chance to win a _____. You must be registered in Summer Reading to enter.

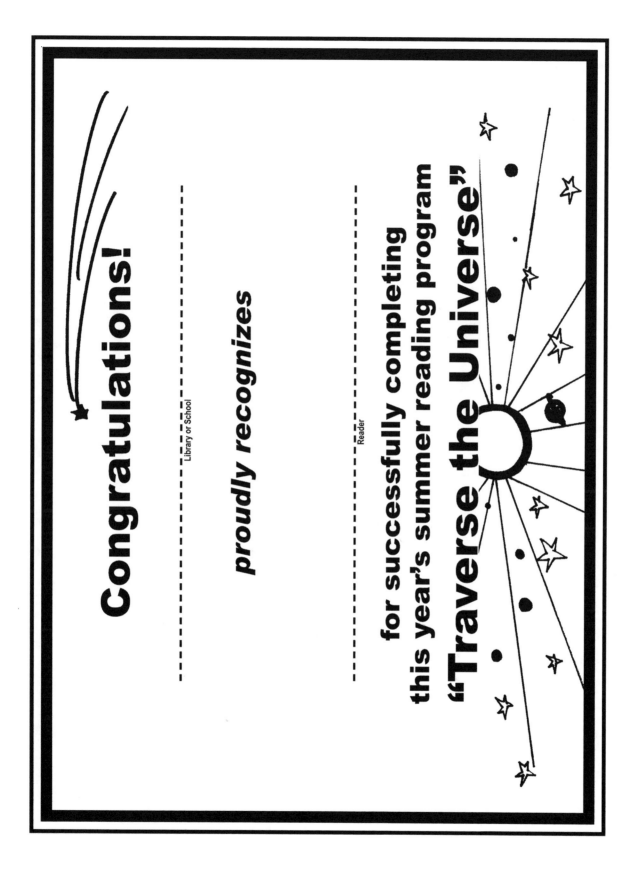

INTERACTIVE CENTER 1

THE BIG BANG THEORY

How Participants Can Interact

Children and adults can explore the theory of the Big Bang and the expansion of the universe by reading the illustrated picture science book *Big Bang! The Tongue-Tickling Tale of a Speck That Became Spectacular* and follow up with a simple balloon exercise.

Materials Needed

Book:

DeCristofano, Carolyn Cinami. 2005. *Big Bang! The Tongue-Tickling Tale of a Speck That Became Spectacular.* Illustrated by Michael Carroll. Watertown, MA: Charlesbridge.

11-inch balloons
Inexpensive handheld balloon inflator
Colored markers

Directions for Participants

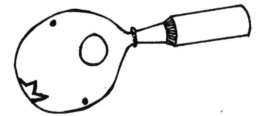

Balloon experiment.

- Read the book *Big Bang! The Tongue-Tickling Tale of a Speck That Became Spectacular* with a parent, friend, or on your own.
- When you are finished reading, pay close attention to page 16.
- Take one balloon and one colored marker.
- Use the balloon inflator to help you inflate the balloon to about the size of an orange.

- Keeping the balloon on the inflator, draw several circles, dots, and stars on the balloon's surface.
- Inflate the balloon to its full size. Stop before it pops!
- Notice how your markings move away from each other as the balloon gets larger, demonstrating how the universe is continually expanding and the galaxies are moving farther away from each other.

Older children may explore the balloon concept at an Internet station set to the following Web site:

NASA Space Place

http://spaceplace.nasa.gov/en/kids/phonedrmarc/2003_june.shtml.
They may also read through the book:

Morgan, Jennifer. 2002. *Born With a Bang: The Universe Tells Our Cosmic Story*, Bk. 1. Nevada City, CA: Dawn Publications.

INTERACTIVE CENTER 2

The Milky Way

Create a Fun Facts display for our galaxy. You may work from a couple of resources listed below or include some of the facts on the reproducible fact sheet. Provide photography either from the resources listed or other available pictures over the Internet to help participants understand the concepts presented in the fun facts.

Resources

Gibbons, Gail. 2007. *Galaxies Galaxies!* New York: Holiday House.
Rau, Dana Meachen. 2005. *The Milky Way and Other Galaxies*. Minneapolis, MN: Compass Point Books.
———. 2005. *Black Holes*. Minneapolis, MN: Compass Point Books.
Windows to the Universe.
    http://www.windows.ucar.edu/tour/link=/the_universe/Milkyway.html&edu=mid
    Provides easily understood information and photographs.
World Book. 2006. *Galaxies and the Universe*. Chicago: World Book.

Milky Way Fun Facts

Spiral galaxy.

- The Milky Way Galaxy is a group of billions of stars, planets, and other objects such as dust and gas.
- The Milky Way contains somewhere between 200 and 400 billion stars.
- On a clear night the Milky Way galaxy looks like a cloudy path.
- The Milky Way got its name from the ancient Greeks for its milky white appearance.
- The shape of the Milky Way is like a large pinwheel with spirals swirling out from its center.
- Earth and our solar system exist on the outer edge of one of the Milky Way's spirals.
- The Italian astronomer Galileo Galilei first thought the milky band of light was actually a group of billions of stars.
- The center of the Milky Way is the brightest and is called "the bulge."
- Within "the bulge" scientists believe there may be a black hole.
- A black hole is an area of space that has a very strong pull of gravity.
- The billions of stars of the Milky Way galaxy are held together by gravity.
- The Milky Way is part of a cluster of other galaxies called the "local group."

From *Summer Reading Renaissance: An Interactive Exhibits Approach* by Rita Soltan. Illustrations by Jill Reichenbach Fill. Westport, CT: Libraries Unlimited. Copyright © 2008.

How Participants Can Interact

Different legends surrounding the Milky Way galaxy are part of various cultures. Two such stories can be on display for reading. Children can then create a Milky Way painting or collage as follows.

Books for Display

Birdseye, Tom. 1990. *A Song of Stars: An Asian Legend.* Illustrated by Ju-Hong Chen. New York: Holiday House.

Bruchac, Joseph, and Gayle Ross. 1995. *The Story of the Milky Way: A Cherokee Tale.* Paintings by Virginia A. Stroud. New York: Dial.

Materials Needed

Sheets of black construction paper
Blue dot stickers
Glue sticks
Bathroom-size paper cups
1- or 2-lb. box of salt
   Have several of the paper cups filled with salt a quarter of the way
Garbage can

Directions for Participants

• Choose one of the stories to read alone, with a parent, or with a friend.

• Take a piece of black construction paper.

Spiral galaxy.

- Using a glue stick, draw an outline of a Milky Way spiral galaxy.
- Using the salt in a paper cup, gently pour the salt over your glue drawing.
- Wait a few minutes for it to dry and then shake off the excess salt into the garbage can.
- Use a blue dot sticker to show where earth's position is on one of the outer spirals.

This activity may also be done using torn cotton balls to create the Milky Way spiral galaxy.

INTERACTIVE CENTER 3

ASTRONOMICAL DISCOVERY

The science of astronomy has been around since ancient times. This center focuses on some of the early astronomers and their discoveries as well as more recent studies done with modern equipment like the Hubble Space Telescope. You may wish to include individual biographies of key astronomers from your collection.

Resources to Have Available and on Display

Morris, Neil. 2003. *Astronomers.* North Mankato, MN: Chrysalis Education/Smart Apple Media.
Sakolsky, Josh. 2005. *Copernicus and Modern Astronomy.* New York: Rosen Publishing Group.
Wills, Susan. 2001. *Astronomy: Looking at the Stars.* Minneapolis, MN: Oliver Press.

Discovery Education
http://school.discovery.com/schooladventures/universe/stargazers/index.html.
Web site to have available at an Internet station:
An exploration with the American Museum of Natural History presents information on early astronomers in a kid-friendly format:
In addition, you may have on hand a poetic pop-up rendition of the universe by J. Patrick Lewis for children to read and explore:

Lewis, J. Patrick. 2005. *Galileo's Universe.* Illustrations by Tom Curry, paper engineering by Bruce Foster. Mankato, MN: Creative Editions.
And a picture book fictitious journal based on Galileo's discoveries:

Pettenatik, Jeanne K. 2006. *Galileo's Journal: 1609–1610.* Boston: Charlesbridge.

How Participants Can Interact

After exploring the Web site and reading the two books featuring Galileo, children can work on a word search puzzle with key astronomers and their discoveries.

THE ASTRONOMER'S
WORD SEARCH

Circle the underlined words in the word search below:

Copernicus was the first astronomer to discover that the movements of the planets revolved around the sun. This was later called the Copernican Revolution.

Galileo was the first astronomer to use a telescope to study the sky.

Isaac Newton developed the law of gravity. The force of gravity keeps the planets, like the moon, in their orbits in the solar system. Gravity also keeps us on earth.

Edmund Halley discovered that stars change positions in space over long periods of time.

Brother and sister scientist team William and Caroline Herschel discovered the planet Uranus.

Edwin Hubble studied galaxies beyond our own Milky Way.

```
A I I N O E S K X M Q U D E R S N Y L B N K
R T J O E L I L A G R E P Z V D T A O D I E
D H A I E C O A U Y T O D P Y I L E S L S S
N E W T O N E N O I C I T E V D O B N K H F
A L H U H R P X S S I Y M A A L C P R A M C
H A L L E Y A M E C C U R C S T I B R O L E
O S N O M Y Z L O L Y G W H O O A S A X N P
R D A V X D E O W M A L D A E B S S C T T J
A H A E V T R H L O W Y V I I R T O T S L L
X C A R S U I K U U Y U M N N S R I S A P P
T N E R R E T E D S K R N G G O O S B O U O
K L E H C S R E H O L A S U C I N R E P O C
C S U R R Y O O D Q I N A N M M O X L L O U
S O L A R S Y S T E M A U K G E O M K J L W
E T E R R S W A A Z V S T A R S E L B B U H
J G A L A X I E S Y E L I A B D R O G C D G
```

THE ASTRONOMER'S WORD SEARCH ANSWERS

INTERACTIVE CENTER 4

AS THE WORLD TURNS

How Participants Can Interact

This center helps children understand how our earth's rotation in space is affected by the moon and sun. Help children visualize the phases of the moon and the earth's orbit around the sun with a visual display.

Web sites to help you create a visual display of the phases of the moon:
NASA Images. Phases of the Moon. http://radiojove.gsfc.nasa.gov/images/phases_of_moon.gif.
Wpclipart. http://www.wpclipart.com/space/illustrations/Moon_Phases.png.
Phases of the Moon. http://www.k111.k12.il.us/king/phases_of_the_moon.htm.

Two nonfiction illustrated books and two poetic renditions can be available at this center for reading and may also serve as a model for your display.

Karas, G. Brian. 2005. *On Earth.* New York: G. Putnam's Sons.
Pollack, Penny. 2001. *When the Moon Is Full.* Boston: Little Brown.
Ryder, Joanne. 1996. *Earth Dance.* Illustrated by Norman Gorbaty. New York: Henry Holt.
Tomecek, Steve. 2005. *Moon.* Illustrated by Liisa Chauncy Guida. Washington, DC: National
    Geographic.

Materials Needed

Moon phases template
Dinner-size white paper plates
Markers, crayons, colored pencils
Ruler
Paper fasteners, scissors

Directions for Participants

- Read one of the books on display with a parent, friend, or on your own.
- Use the books and the illustrations to help you with this activity.

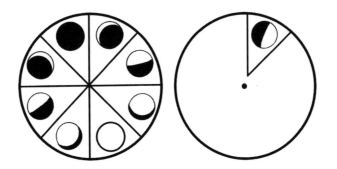

Moon phase activity.

Phases of the Moon

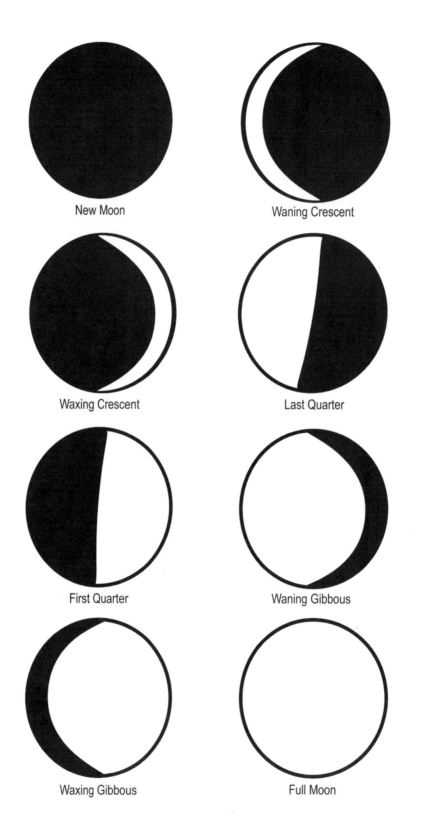

New Moon

Waning Crescent

Waxing Crescent

Last Quarter

First Quarter

Waning Gibbous

Waxing Gibbous

Full Moon

- Take two paper plates.
- Divide one plate into 8 equal parts by folding the plate in half 3 different times.
  - Fold the plate in half.
  - With the fold in place fold the plate in half again so the straight edges touch.
  - Fold the plate one more time so the straight edges touch once again.
  - Open the plate to 8 equal portions.
- Using the template, draw the phases of the moon in each of the 8 sections and label them.
- Take the other plate and cut out one of the eight sections using your first plate as a guide.
- Put the two plates together, front to back, and fasten them in the center with a paper fastener (have an adult help you make a small hole).
- Move your open plate to show the various phases of the moon.

Unit 2 The Library Planetarium

If you are fortunate enough to have a planetarium in your community, you may contact them through their education director to work out a cooperative way to include them in your summer library program. A planetarium display in your library can include anything from hanging huge commercially prepared posters about the planets and solar system to creating your own version with your local museum's assistance.

Resources to Help You Create a Solar System Display

Brenner, Barbara. 2002. *Planetarium.* Illustrated by Ron Miller. New York: Ipicturebooks.com. This is available as an electronic book from the 1993 edition published by Bantam Books. The author provides facts about each planet through a planetarium-style tour.
Croswell, Ken. 2006. *Ten Worlds: Everything That Orbits the Sun.* Honesdale, PA: Boyds Mills Press.
Jenkins, Alvin. 2004. *Next Stop Neptune: Experiencing the Solar System.* Illustrated by Steve Jenkins. Boston: Houghton Mifflin.

Web Sites

Hands On Crafts For Kids
    http://www.craftsforkids.com/projects/real_solar_system.htm.
MountKolias: Mountains of Information on How to do Anything
    http://www.kolias.com/education/solarsystem.htm.
Pacific Beach Elementary
    http://www.buddies.org/PacBeach/giggl6.html.

INTERACTIVE CENTER 1

Virtual Ride through the Solar System

How Participants Can Interact

This center can be developed to use the Internet using webquests that you create or may offer through a portal such as http://www.webquest.org/, hosted by San Diego

State University. An excellent example of a solar system interactive webquest created by teacher Laurel Anderson can be found at:

http://users.zoominternet.net/~eanderson/webquest/index.html.

Here, children and parents are led to a variety of both informational and interactive Web sites to explore the planets and solar system in a carefully and well-organized quest.

Another Web site that offers your summer readers a virtual view of the sky is Your Sky, created by John Walker, founder of Autodesk, Inc. and coauthor of AutoCAD:

http://www.fourmilab.ch/yoursky/.

This free-to-use Web site allows participants to explore the sky, the planetary, and constellation positions from their home city.

Finally, Amazing Space, an award-winning Web site found at http://amazing-space.stsci.edu/, also virtually explores the night sky month by month. Children can explore the stars and planets as they would appear in a planetarium show with a voice-over explanation. The site is maintained and designed by the Formal Education Group of the Space Telescope Science Institute's Office of Public Outreach.

Books for Display

Alberti, Theresa Jarosz. 2004. *Out and About at the Planetarium.* Minneapolis, MN: Picture Window Books.

Claybourne, Anna. 2006. *The Solar System.* New York: Chelsea House.

Cole, Joanna, and Bruce Degen. 1990. *The Magic School Bus Lost in the Solar System.* New York: Scholastic.

Davis, Kenneth C. 2001. *Don't Know Much about the Solar System.* Illustrated by Pedro Martin. New York: HarperCollins.

Gibbons, Gail. 2005. *The Planets.* Rev. ed. New York: Holiday House.

Simon, Seymour. 2007. *Our Solar System.* Rev. ed. New York: HarperCollins.

More Webquest Resources

Internet 4 Classrooms: Helping Teachers Use the Internet Effectively. WebQuests. http://www.internet4classrooms.com/on-line_quest.htm.

INTERACTIVE CENTER 2

FLYING OBJECTS IN SPACE

This center focuses on asteroids, comets, meteors, and other flying objects in space. Create an exhibit briefly explaining the difference between the various objects mentioned. A simple comparison can be found on page 132–33 of *The Kids Book of the Night Sky* by Ann Love and Jane Drake (see resources list for this unit).

A good viewing sample can be found at the New York American Museum of Natural History's Cosmic Collisions Web site, which has a short, 1 1/2 minute video clip. Key information based on the show is available for educators and children alike at:

http://www.amnh.org/rose/spaceshow/cosmic/.

The BBC Web site, BBC Science and Nature: Space, includes easily read and understood information on comets and asteroids in addition to some nifty interactive puzzles and game possibilities:

http://www.bbc.co.uk/science/space/solarsystem/index.shtml.

Meteor Multiplication

Work this problem out with paper and pencil
or use dry beans to count out the number of meteors per second.

40 per second x 10 seconds = 400

Extra Challenge:

How many would you see in one minute?

How many would you see in five minutes?

From *Summer Reading Renaissance: An Interactive Exhibits Approach* by Rita Soltan. Illustrations by Jill Reichenbach Fill. Westport, CT: Libraries Unlimited. Copyright © 2008.

Resources to Have Available for This Display

Hans, E. M. 2001. *Comets and Asteroids.* New York: Raintree Steck-Vaughn.
    Good clear photography for display table.
Koppes, Steven N. 2004. *Killer Rocks From Outer Space: Asteroids, Comets, and Meteorites.* Minneapolis, MN: Lerner.
Nicolson, Cynthia. 1999. *Comets, Asteroids, and Meteorites.* Illustrated by Bill Slavin. Toronto: Kids Can Press.
    Concepts are organized for easy fact sheet/bulletin board informational display.
Rau, Dana Meachen. 2003. *Comets, Asteroids, and Meteoroids.* Minneapolis, MN: Compass Point Books.

How Participants Can Interact

Participants can read a science-oriented illustrated story about a little girl watching a meteor shower and do one of the activities presented on the "Creative Minds" page at the end of the book.

Materials Needed

Book:

Rockliff, Mara. 2005. *Pieces of Another World.* Illustrated by Salima Alikhan. Mt. Pleasant, SC: Sylvan Dell Publishing.

Meteor Math is a simple multiplication exercise that can be done as the directions indicate.
Children may work out the problem with paper and pencil or use dry beans to count out the number of meteors per second.

INTERACTIVE CENTER 3

WHAT ABOUT PLUTO?

The controversy over Pluto's status as the ninth planet is an exhibit you may create with the help of articles and information found online from the magazine *Science News for Kids.* The link below opens to a recent article that includes access to other explanations and a teacher's resource question guide on the subject.

Sohn, Emily. 2007. "Defining Planethood." *Science News for Kids Magazine.* http://www.science newsforkids.org/articles/20070228/Feature1.asp.

How Participants Can Interact

The above article offers a way for kids to vote online if they believe Pluto should be considered one of the planets in our solar system. You may print out the article and have copies available. In addition, create a display with key bullet points extrapolated from the article and a voting box with a check-off ballot sheet for kids to mark.

Set up your polling area right next to your exhibit on Pluto. Allow voting to take place for the length of your exhibit. At the end of the voting period, take a count and display the results.

You may also invite a science teacher or local planetarium educator to offer a discussion group on a particular day or evening to further explore this topic after or before your voting takes place.

Resources to Help You Create a Display on Pluto

Hayhurst, Chris. 2005. *Pluto.* New York: Rosen Publishing.
    Pages 33–36 include "The Great Debate: Is Pluto Really a Planet?"
Potts, Steve. 2004. *Pluto.* North Mankato, MN: Smart Apple Media.
Scott, Elaine. 2007. *When Is a Planet Not a Planet? The Story of Pluto.* New York: Clarion.
Tocci, Salvatore. 2003. *A Look at Pluto.* New York: Franklin Watts.
World Book. 2006. *Neptune and Pluto.* Chicago: World Book.

Vote for Pluto

Materials Needed

Closed cardboard box with an opening cut out at top for ballots
(you may decorate the box with solar system graphics, etc.)
Voting ballot from template
Pencils

Unit 3 Sky Lore

This unit offers the mythology and astrology of the planets and constellations and includes a writing center for children to do their own creative writing with poetry, simple stories, book making, and even an online zine or wiki managed through your library's web page.

Resources for This Unit

Galat, Joan Marie. 2002. *Dot to Dot in the Sky: Stories in the Stars.* North Vancouver: Whitecap Books.
Kerrod, Robin. 2003. *Starwatch: A Month-By-Month Guide to the Night Sky.* Hauppauge, New York: Barron's Educational Series.

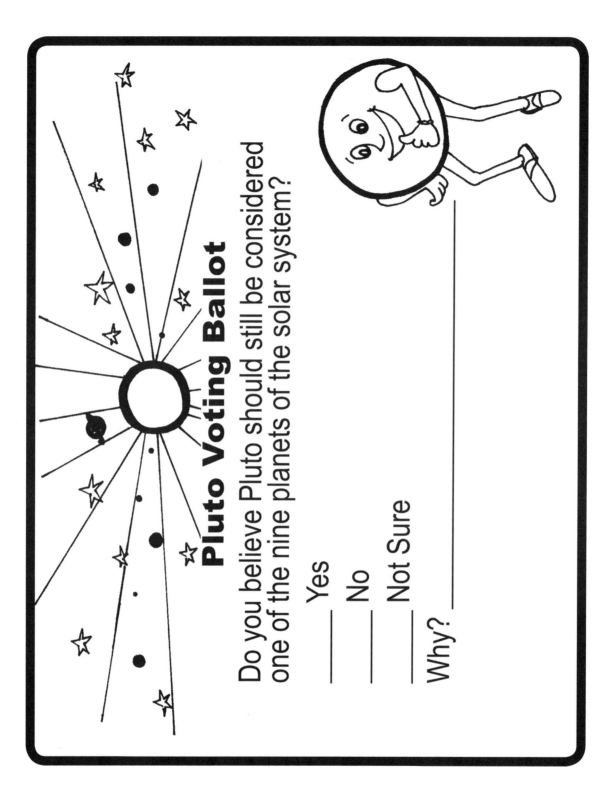

Pluto Voting Ballot

Do you believe Pluto should still be considered one of the nine planets of the solar system?

_____ Yes

_____ No

_____ Not Sure

Why? _____

Rau, Dana Meachen. 2005. *Constellations.* Minneapolis, MN: Compass Point Books.
Sasaki, Chris. 2002. *Constellations: The Stars and Stories.* Illustrations by Joe Boddy. New York: Sterling Publishing Co.
Scagell, Robin. 2004. *Children's Night Sky Atlas.* London: Dorling Kindersley.

INTERACTIVE CENTER 1

STAR SEARCH

How Participants Can Interact

Make available several short yet information-filled illustrated nonfiction picture books as an introduction to the constellations in the sky. A dot-to-dot reproducible sheet can be given out for children to complete with some of the summer constellations that appear in our northern sky. In addition, you may refer to the following book for additional ideas on creating center content:

Van Cleave, Janice. 1997. *Janice VanCleave's Constellations for Every Kid: Easy Activities That Make Learning Science Fun.* New York: John Wiley & Sons.

NASA: The Space Place offers free downloadable and printable star-finder pattern sheets for each month of the year:

http://spaceplace.nasa.gov/en/kids/st6starfinder/st6starfinder.shtml.

Materials Needed

Books:

Branley, Franklyn M. 1983. *The Sky is Full of Stars.* Illustrated by Felicia Bond. New York: HarperCollins.
Gibbons, Gail. 1992. *Stargazers.* New York: Holiday House.
Mackall, Dandi Daley. 2006. *Seeing Stars.* Illustrated by Claudine Gevry. New York: Little Simon.
Rockwell, Anne. 1999. *Our Stars.* San Diego: Harcourt Brace & Company.
Tomecek, Steve. 2003. *Stars.* Illustrated by Sachiko Yoshikawa. Washington, DC: National Geographic.

Reproducible Dot-to-Dot Summer Constellations sheet
Colored pencils or crayons

Directions for Participants

Read one of the books on display.
Use the Dot-to-Dot sheet to draw out the summer constellations and the "Who Am I" clues below each one to complete its imagined shape.

Dot-To-Dot Summer Constellations #1
"Who Am I?"

I am a Swan

I am also known as the Northern Cross

My brightest star is Deneb, meaning tail in Arabic

My beak is the star Albireo

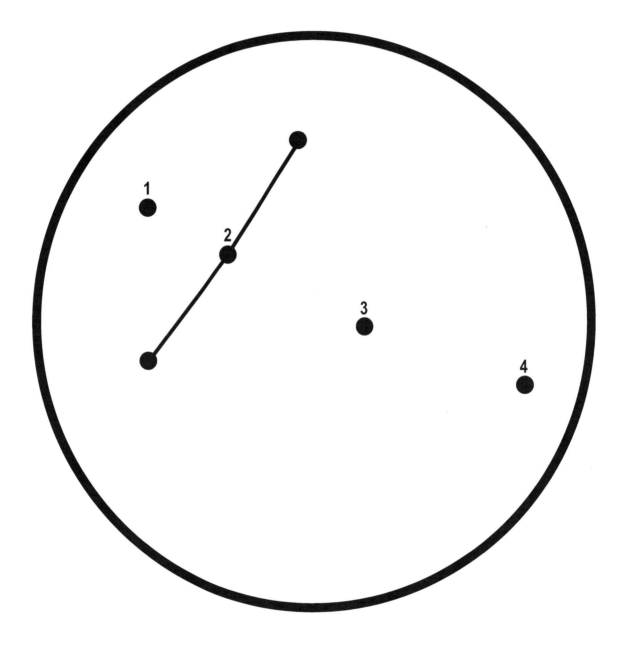

Dot-To-Dot Summer Constellations #2
"Who Am I?"

I am an Eagle

I am the second flying bird to Cygnus

I am formed with the brilliant star Altair

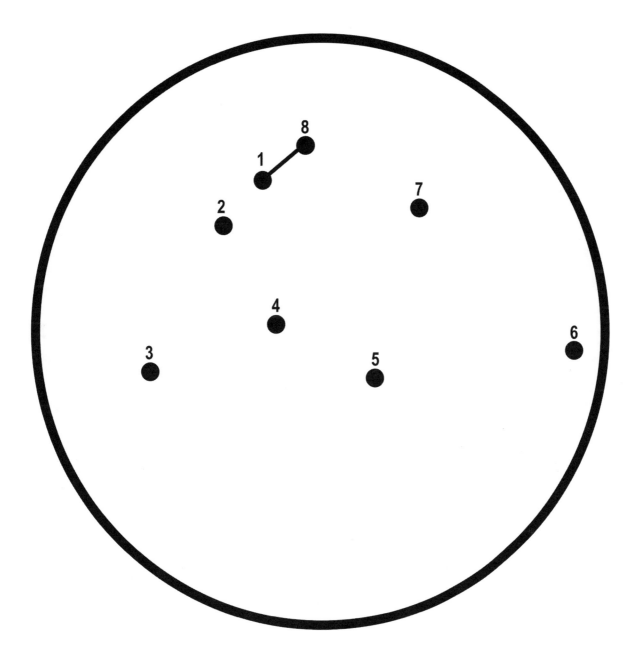

Dot-To-Dot Summer Constellations #3
"Who Am I?"

I am a Lyre, a small string instrument

Mercury invented me

I am dominated by the fifth brightest star, Vega

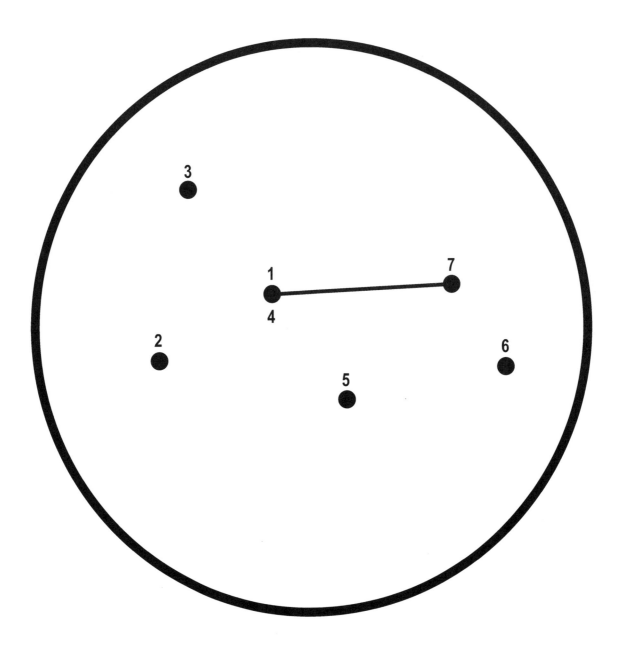

Dot-To-Dot Summer Constellations #4
"Who Am I?"

I am a Scorpion

I can be seen best in June

I killed the mighty hunter Orion

My brightest star Antares is the center of my shell

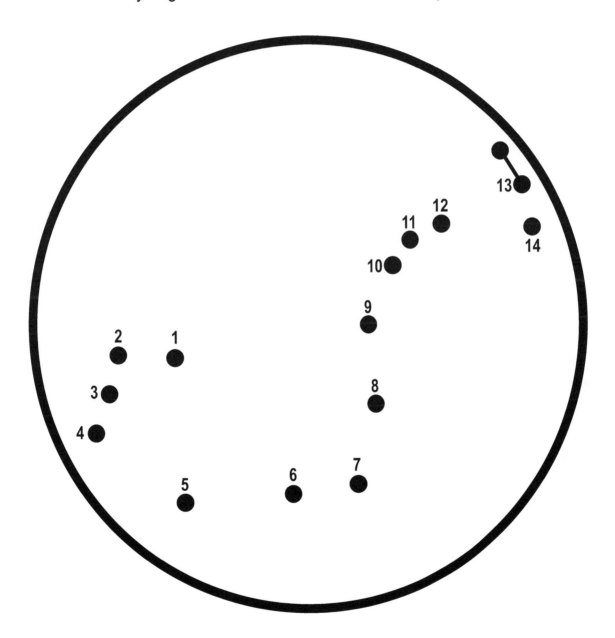

From *Summer Reading Renaissance: An Interactive Exhibits Approach* by Rita Soltan. Illustrations by Jill Reichenbach Fill. Westport, CT: Libraries Unlimited. Copyright © 2008.

Dot-To-Dot Summer Constellations #5
"Who Am I?"

I am an Archer

I am in the brightest part of the Milky Way

I sometimes look like a teapot in the summer sky

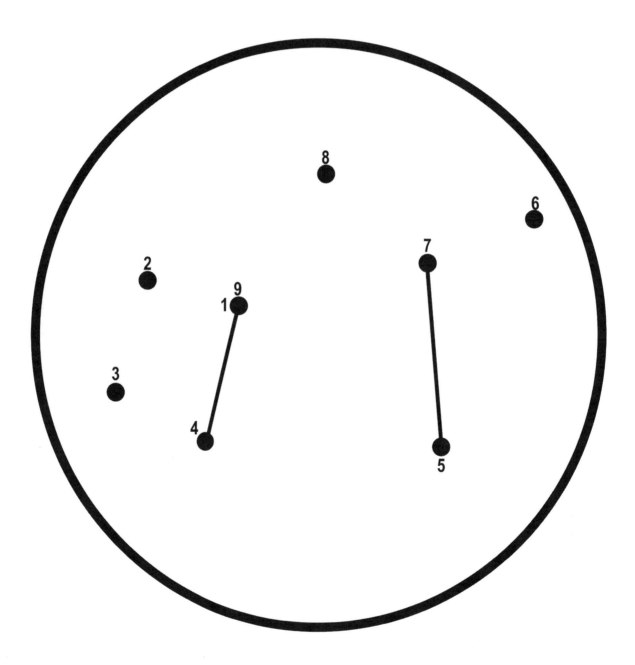

INTERACTIVE CENTER 2

NAME THAT PLANET

The planets have been named after the mythological Greek and Roman gods. Create a display board indicating the name and meaning behind each planet's name. Two Web sites, the first offered by NASA and the second by Pearson Education, can help you with key information:

http://starchild.gsfc.nasa.gov/docs/StarChild/questions/question48.html.
http://www.factmonster.com/ipka/A0875452.html.

Books to Consult

Ashworth, Leon. 2003. *Gods and Goddesses of Ancient Rome.* North Mankato, MN: Smart Apple Media.

Asimov, Isaac. 1990. *Mythology and the Universe.* Milwaukee, WI: Gareth Stevens.

You may also create a characteristics sheet about the Roman and Greek gods and goddesses and their corresponding planet names from the reproducible sample below.

Children can refer to two books for information on the corresponding Greek and Roman gods:

Aliki. 1994. *The Gods and Goddesses of Olympus.* New York: HarperCollins.

Woff, Richard. 2003. *A Pocket Dictionary of Greek and Roman Gods and Goddesses.* Los Angeles: The J. Paul Getty Museum.

Mythology behind the Planets

The word *planets* comes from the Greek meaning "wanders." As people in ancient Greece and Rome watched the planets move through the sky, they gave them names to match the qualities of their gods and goddesses. Many of the ancient Greek gods had similar counterparts in the ancient Roman world. To this day, we use the Roman names for the planets in our solar system.

Roman God	Mythical Quality	Planet Feature
Venus	Goddess of Beauty	Brightest in sky
Mars	God of War	Red, color of blood
Mercury	Messenger of Gods	Fastest moving
Saturn	God of Agriculture	Slowest moving
Jupiter	King of the Gods	Largest in sky
Neptune	God of the Sea	Sea blue/green in color
Uranus	God of the Sky	Neptune's twin, blue/green in color
Pluto	God of the Underworld	Darkest and farthest from our sun

Venus

Mythical Quality: Goddess of Beauty
Planet Feature: Brightest in sky

Mars

Mythical Quality: God of War
Planet Feature: Red, color of blood

Mercury

Mythical Quality: Messenger of Gods
Planet Feature: Fastest moving

Saturn

Mythical Quality: God of Agriculture
Planet Feature: Slowest moving

From *Summer Reading Renaissance: An Interactive Exhibits Approach* by Rita Soltan. Illustrations by Jill Reichenbach Fill. Westport, CT: Libraries Unlimited. Copyright © 2008.

Jupiter

Mythical Quality: **King of the Gods**

Planet Feature: **Largest in sky**

Neptune

Mythical Quality: **God of the Sea**

Planet Feature: **Sea blue/green in color**

Uranus

Mythical Quality: **God of the Sky**

Planet Feature: **Neptune's twin, blue/green in color**

Pluto

Mythical Quality: **God of the Underworld**

Planet Feature: **Darkest and farthest from our sun**

How Participants Can Interact

One of the best-told and illustrated Roman myths is *Daughter of Earth*, by Gerald McDermott. After reading this story children can create a mosaic wall of the characters/gods in the story.

Materials Needed

Book:

McDermott, Gerald. 1984. *Daughter of Earth: A Roman Myth.* New York: Delacorte Press. (Since this book is out of print and may be unavailable, you can also use a story from a more recent collection: McCaughrean, Geraldine. 1999. *Roman Myths.* Illustrated by Emma Chichester Clark. New York: Margaret K. McElderry Books.)

Large piece of craft paper prominently hung in an area accessible to children
Assorted construction paper
Pencils
Ruler
Assorted colored markers
Scissors
Glue sticks or white glue and cotton swabs
Double-sided tape
Copies of character templates

Directions for Participants

- Choose one of the character templates.
- With the ruler and pencil lightly divide the drawing into four horizontal and vertical lines so your drawing looks like a checkerboard with 10 squares.
- With the colored markers, color each of the 10 squares with different colors to decorate your character.
- Carefully cut along the lines, placing the pieces down in order.
- Glue the mosaic pieces down on a piece of construction paper to recreate the mosaic of your character.
- Carefully cut a rectangular frame around your mosaic.
- Finished dry mosaics can be hung on the brown craft paper with double-sided tape for a mosaic wall of Roman gods and characters in the myth *Daughter of Earth.*

Resources for Creating Mosaic Art

Freixenet, Anna. 2000. *Creating with Mosaics.* Woodbridge, CT: Blackbirch Press.
Kelly, Sarah. 2000. *Amazing Mosaics.* Hauppauge, NY: Barrons.
Powell, Michelle. 2001. *Step-by-Step Mosaics.* Chicago: Heinemann Library.

Mosaic Character Templates

Jupiter, King of the Sky

Pluto, King of the Dead

Ceres, Goddess of Earth

Proserpina, Daughter of Earth

Mercury, Fleet-Footed Messenger

Sol the Sun

Pomegranate

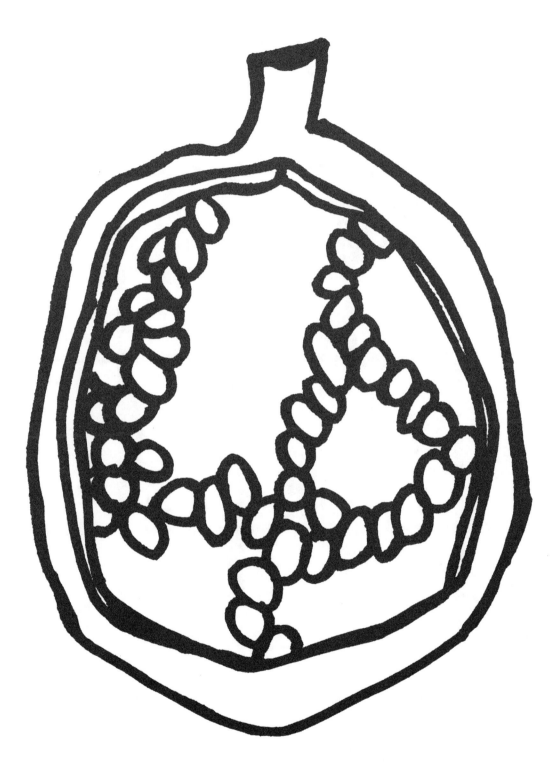

From *Summer Reading Renaissance: An Interactive Exhibits Approach* by Rita Soltan. Illustrations by Jill Reichenbach Fill. Westport, CT: Libraries Unlimited. Copyright © 2008.

INTERACTIVE CENTER 3
WRITING CENTER

This center can be as simple as providing opportunities for creative writing with sample templates. Finished work may be displayed around your room or bound in a zine. You may wish to develop an online collaborative anthology of original writing through the library's Web site with an e-zine or wiki. Encourage children to write and illustrate their work as well.

A Word or Two on Poetry

Introducing and incorporating poetry in your writing center is a way to reopen the door to literary creativity through both an emotional and intelligent response. After reading a good poem a person may feel pleasure, interest, happiness, sadness, or any other range of emotions. Poetry opens the way for children to listen to themselves and for adults to listen to children so that their personal experiences are heard and valued. Poems can provide a child comfort, laughter, happy or sad memories, self-awareness, or a cognizance of the surrounding world. They also help a child to express him- or herself through sensory and visual experiences by making observations in both a critical and creative way. An easy way to encourage children to write poetry is to allow them the freedom to write in free verse style. Free verse does not have to rhyme yet functions through a combination of cadence, rhythm, and form layout on a page. Helping children understand and create other forms of poetry such as cinquains, acrostics, or haikus can be done by using templates (see below) with examples they can follow. In addition, a fun poetic format known as the concrete poem, which involves the shape of the poem created by the words, can be explored in this area. Use the following general books on poetry by Paul Janeczko to help you develop this poetry area.

Janeczko, Paul. 1999. *How to Write Poetry.* New York: Scholastic.
   A general resource tool for children and adults.
———. 2001. *A Poke in the I: A Collection of Concrete Poems.* Illustrated by Chris Raschka. Cambridge, MA: Candlewick Press, 2001.
———. 2005. *A Kick in the Head: An Everyday Guide to Poetic Forms.* Illustrated by Chris Raschka. Cambridge, MA: Candlewick Press.
   Illustrates and explains the different forms of poetry, including sonnet, couplet, ballad, elegy, and ode.

Space Poetry Books for viewing and reading:

Florian, Douglas. 2007. *Comets, Stars, the Moon, and Mars: Space Poems and Paintings.* New York: Harcourt.
Hopkins, Lee Bennett, ed. 1995. *Blast Off! Poems About Space.* Illustrated by Melissa Sweet. New York: HarperCollins.
Peddicord, Jane Ann. 2005. *Night Wonders.* Watertown, MA: Charlesbridge.
Whitman, Walt. 2004. *When I Heard the Learn'd Astronomer.* Pictures by Loren Long. New York: Simon & Schuster.

Poetry Templates

Cinquain

A Cinquain contains 22 syllables distributed as a 2, 4, 6, 8, 2 pattern in 5 lines.

Title (2 syllables)	*Sun Star*
Description of title (4 syllables)	*Blazing and hot*
Expressing action (6 syllables)	*Brightens and warms the earth*
Expressing feeling (8 syllables)	*Sunny, happy, blissful, gleaming*
Synonym for the title (2 syllables)	*Star glow*

Write Your Own Cosmic Cinquain

_____

_____

_____

_____

Acrostic

An acrostic poem uses the letters in a word as the starting point for each line.

Space is the planets and the stars
Universe is all there is
Near and light-years away from us

Write an acrostic poem for the word SPACE. Your poem does not have to rhyme!

S_____

P_____

A_____

C_____

E_____

Choose another word for your space poem and write your own acrostic.

From *Summer Reading Renaissance: An Interactive Exhibits Approach* by Rita Soltan. Illustrations by Jill Reichenbach Fill. Westport, CT: Libraries Unlimited. Copyright © 2008.

Haiku

The most popular Japanese style of poetry, haiku emphasizes natural beauty. The general format is a three-line poem with a total of 17 syllables that work as:

line one = 5 syllables, line two = 7 syllables, line three = 5 syllables.

Sun's blistering shine
Lights and warms earth's atmosphere
Radiant brilliance

Write a haiku for your favorite planet, constellation, or anything in the universe! Remember to illustrate your poem.

Summer Reading Zines

A wonderful way to encourage kids to write, illustrate, and generally create their own literary content is to produce a summer reading zine. Zines are homemade pamphlets or magazines that offer a variety of printed formats, from stories and poetry to personal essays and comic or graphic pieces. By providing a specific theme—such as Traverse the Universe—and a few guidelines, together with a "staff" of volunteer boosters (see chapter 4) to edit, design layout, reproduce, and bind under your general direction, children can feel a sense of accomplishment in developing a community-wide summer-long project. Look for these books to help you start and organize your summer reading zine.

Block, Francesca Lia, and Hilary Carlip. 1998. *Zine Scene.* Chicago, Girl Press.
Todd, Mark, and Esther Pearl Watson. 2006. *Whatcha Mean, What's a Zine? The Art of Making Zines and Mini-Comics.* Boston: Graphia/Houghton, Mifflin.
Wrekk, Alex. 2005. *Stolen Sharpie Revolution: A DIY Zine Resource.* Portland, OR: Microcosm.

Publish on the Web

Your collaborative publishing can also be targeted to produce a web-based anthology of your summer readers' literary efforts through your library's Web site. Possibilities range from simply uploading digital images and documents to a summer reading page set aside on your library's youth link to developing and maintaining a controlled, password-protected wiki (an online writing space for children to use in a collaborative way) for your summer reading creative writing center. You can research possibilities and ways to implement certain web-based ideas for this kind of technologically shared concept through several books dedicated to library and school Web site design and maintenance that offer opportunities for Internet-related programming and teaching.

Blowers, Helene, and Robin Bryan. 2004. *Weaving a Library Web: A Guide to Developing Children's Websites.* Chicago: ALA Editions.
    The authors provide concrete and comprehensive information on offering engaging online activities for children through a library's Web site. Developing and maintaining a site is supplemented with good advice on special considerations such as privacy, gaining parental permission for any personal work to be uploaded and displayed, building a project team to help create content for a children's digital library service, and online summer reading program ideas.
Logan, Debra Kay, and Cynthia Lee Beuselinck. 2002. *K–12 Web Pages: Planning and Publishing Excellent School Web Sites.* Worthington, OH: Linworth.
    While this book is targeted at schools and educational purposes, chapter 4, "Blueprints for a Firm Foundation: Publishing Guidelines and Policies," can help you keep your summer readers safe and your library's liability and responsibility within a framework that promotes a secure online environment.
Richardson, Will. 2006. *Blogs, Wikis, Podcasts, and Other Powerful Web Tools for Classrooms.* Thousand Oaks, CA: Corwin Press.
    Chapter 4 provides solid advice and how-to information on creating and maintaining wikis for student populations.

Smith, Susan Sharpless. 2006. *Web-Based Instruction: A Guide for Libraries.* 2nd ed. Chicago: American Library Association.
>This updated edition provides a section on different ways to provide "interactivity," including weblogs and wikis.

Also, the Web site Internet 4 Classrooms offers links to understanding and working with wikis at:
>Internet 4 Classrooms. Web 2.0. http://www.internet4classrooms.com/web2.htm.

Unit 4 Space Exploration

Exploring the worlds beyond our atmosphere has intrigued humanity for thousands of years but has been a reality for only the last 50 years. This unit provides a glimpse into the past, present, and future of space exploration with books, online games, software, and imaginary space arts and crafts possibilities.

INTERACTIVE CENTER 1

DID YOU KNOW?

Space exploration trivia can be offered in numerous ways, both at a center created with an interactive question-and-answer board or with some well-designed online trivia games offered by National Geographic and NASA. PowerPoint can be a terrific tool to use to create your own jeopardy or trivia-type game. Help on creating a simple game can be found online at several teacher help sites. One of the best is offered by Kim Overstreet, District Technology Resource Teacher at the Fayette County Public Schools in Lexington, Kentucky at:
>http://teach.fcps.net/trt10/PowerPoint.htm.

Here you can learn how to use PowerPoint for your trivia game, how to incorporate questions and answers, and how to set up your game at a computer center.

In addition, free downloads for templates, including a solar system planets template, can be found at:
>http://www.templateready.com/Specials/Free_educational_template.html.

Make Up Your Questions for Your Game from Information in These Resources

Berger, Melvin, and Gilda Berger. 2000. *Can You Hear a Shout in Space?* New York: Scholastic.
Casanellas, Antonio. 2000. *Great Discoveries and Inventions That Helped Explore Earth and Space.* Milwaukee, WI: Gareth Stevens.
Kobasa, Paul A., ed. 2005. *Human Space Exploration.* World Book's Solar System and Space Exploration Library. Chicago: World Book, Inc.

You can also offer a second computer bookmarked to these online trivia sites:

NASA. Observatorium Space Trivia.
>http://observe.arc.nasa.gov/nasa/fun/space_trivia/space_trivia.html.
National Geographic. Exploring Space.
>http://magma.nationalgeographic.com/ngm/space/trivia.html.

INTERACTIVE CENTER 2

FROM THE MOON TO MARS AND A SPACE STATION IN BETWEEN

Children can imagine their own space exploration through the reading of several books available at this center.

Younger children can read or listen to:

Leedy, Loreen. 1993. *Postcards from Pluto: A Tour of the Solar System.* New York: Holiday House.
Suen, Anastasia. 1997. *Man on the Moon.* Illustrated by Benrei Huang. New York: Viking.

Older children can read or browse through:

Halpern, Paul. 2004. *Faraway Worlds: Planets beyond Our Solar System.* Illustrated by Lynette R. Cook. Watertown, MA: Charlesbridge.
Leedy, Loreen, and Andre Schuerger. 2006. *Messages from Mars.* New York: Holiday House.

Send Your Own Message from Space

Children can create their own imagined message from space, which can then be displayed on a bulletin board set aside for this purpose.

Email Template

Message from Space

TO:

FROM:

UNIVERSE LOCATION:

SPECIAL MESSAGE:

Materials Needed

Email Message template
Crayons, colored pencils, markers
Bulletin board

Directions for Participants

- Read one of the books on display.
- Imagine yourself on an exploration in outer space.
- Write a message to your friends or family on what you have discovered.
- Illustrate your message and place it on the message board for others to view.

Take a Tour of the International Space Station

The editors of *YES Magazine* have written a book that allows kids to explore and even experiment a bit to experience life and work aboard the International Space Station:

Kids Can Press. 2003. *The Amazing International Space Station.* Illustrated by Rose Cowles. Tonawanda, NY: Kids Can Press.

Children can read and browse through this easy format filled with bright color photography. The book offers several easy-to-recreate experiments such as growing crystals (page 33) to illustrate scientific studies in microgravity. You can choose to set up a crystal-growing area for children to watch throughout the summer.

An Internet site that offers children a virtual Space Station experience can be found at:

http://www.discovery.com/stories/science/iss/iss.html.

INTERACTIVE CENTER 3

OUT OF THIS WORLD: ALIENS, EXTRATERRESTRIALS, AND OTHER SPACE CREATURES

While no one knows if life exists on other planets, our imagination can conjure up all sorts of possibilities. Two science fiction picture books can be available for reading at this center, followed by a writing and art activity. Finished projects should be displayed for viewing throughout the youth room.

Suggested Books:

Scieszka, Jon, and Lane Smith. 2001. *Baloney (Henry P.).* New York: Viking.
Van Allsburg, Chris. 2002. *Zathura: A Space Adventure.* Boston: Houghton Mifflin.

Write Your Own Alien Tale
Materials Needed

Pencil and paper.

Writing paper
Construction paper
Crayons, assorted pencils, markers

Drawing Books:

Fischel, Emma, and Anita Ganeri. 1988. *How to Draw Spacecraft.* London: Usborne.
Hart, Christopher. 2002. *Mecha Mania: How to Draw the Battling Robots, Cool Spaceships, and Military Vehicles of Japanese Comics.* New York: Watson-Guptill.
Walsh, Patricia. 2001. *Draw It! Space Vehicles.* Chicago: Heinemann.

Directions for Participants

- Read the book *Baloney (Henry P.)* on your own, or with a friend or parent.
- Henry P. Baloney has his own list of words to tell his own story.
- Use some of the "decoder" words at the end of the story to write your own alien tale.
- Make up a few "alien words" for your tale.
- Illustrate your story.
- Use the drawing books at the center as a guide to illustrate your story.

Craft a Space Adventure

This activity can be designed around several craft-oriented space-themed books. Children can read the Van Allsburg story and create their own aliens, planet models, etc. Three books that can help you develop specific craft ideas are:

Biddle, Steve and Megumi. 1998. *Planet Origami: Cosmic Paper Folding for Kids.* Hauppauge, NY: Barron's.
    Provides paper-folding instructions for creating a collection of cosmic items, including stars, planets, a Milky Way Galaxy, an alien, and more.
Boekhoff, P. M. 2007. *Nifty Thrifty Space Crafts.* Berkley Heights, NJ: Enslow.
    Simple space-oriented craft projects including space vehicles and astronomical models.
Ross, Kathy. 1997. *Crafts for Kids Who Are Wild about Outer Space.* Illustrated by Sharon Lane Holm. Brookfield, CT: Millbrook.
    Younger-oriented projects such as a "Straw Rocket" or an egg carton "Moon Buggy" are featured.

Materials Needed

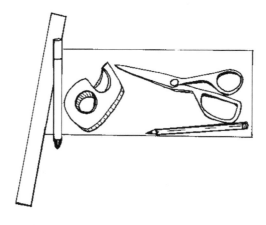

Craft supplies.

Various, depending on projects chosen to highlight for this center

Directions for Participants

- Read the book *Zathura* on your own, with a friend, or with a parent.
- The characters, Walter and Danny, encounter several celestial creatures and outer space phenomena.
- Imagine yourself in a space adventure and create one of the projects sampled at the table.

Add Pizzazz to Traverse the Universe

During portions of the two-week unit periods, event programming can be planned to include any of the following ideas:

Extra Terrestrials Costume Party

Turn your community room or children's library into an alien night complete with a costume parade, alien stories, and, of course, out-of-this-world treats.

Spaced-Out Poetry Slam

Branch out from the writing center and hold an evening poetry reading. Continue your program virtually with a digital video recording and post it on the library's Web site.

Stories in the Sky Festival

Hire a storyteller or encourage local high school forensics students and competition winners to participate in a family-oriented evening of space and constellation mythological storytelling.

The Pluto Debate

Unveil the results of the Pluto ballot and hold a debate between two local authorities, perhaps science teachers or astronomy buffs.

Annotated Bibliography for Related Traverse the Universe Fiction
For the Preschool Crowd

Bartram, Simon. 2002. *Man on the Moon (A Day in the Life of Bob)*. Cambridge, MA: Candlewick.
Bob has the unusual job of being the custodian of the moon, cleaning up after each day's interplanetary tourists and even running the gift shop. A quirky look at a futuristic occupation.

Cushman, Doug. 2004. *Space Cat*. New York: HarperCollins.
When astronaut Space Cat and his robot, Earl withstand a meteor attack that damages their fuel tank, they crash land on an alien planet in search of help. A Beginning Reader book.

Elliott, David. 2004. *Hazel Nutt, Alien Hunter*. New York: Holiday House.
Puns and silly antics abound in this space travel spoof about alien hunter Hazel Nutt, her ship *BoobyPrize*, and the "Meateor" (meatballs) shower they encounter.

Faller, Regis. 2006. *The Adventures of Polo*. New Milford, CT: Roaring Brook Press.
A wordless adventure that has a smart little pup traveling far and wide across the universe, experiencing everything from a volcanic eruption to a lunar escapade.

Keats, Ezra Jack. 1981. *Regards to the Man in the Moon*. New York: Four Winds Press.
The classic picture book about the neighborhood kids who build a space ship from Louie's foster father's junk pile and name it *IMAGINATION I*.

McNulty, Faith. 2005. *If You Decide to Go to the Moon*. New York: Scholastic.
An engaging travel guide to a space trip to the moon for young readers ready to embark on a lunar adventure.

Milgrim, David. 2007. *Another Day in the Milky Way*. New York: G.P. Putnam's Sons.
Waking on the wrong planet one morning, Monty spends the day trying to find a way back home, succeeding with the eventual help of the wise Starman on the Hill.

Yaccarino, Dan. 1997. *Zoom! Zoom! Zoom! I'm Off to the Moon!* New York: Scholastic Press.
A boy in his space ship takes a rhyming, adventurous trip to the moon.

Yang, James. 2006. *Joey and Jet in Space*. New York: Atheneum.
In a backyard imaginative-play scenario, Jet, Joey's dog, flies off into space to chase a bone, while Joey searches by asking planets, space ships, the moon, and satellites if they have seen his missing dog.

For Older Readers

Ball, Justin, and Evan Croker. 2006. *Space Dogs*. New York: Knopf. Grades 5–8.
Off-the-wall science fiction comedy featuring the descendants of the first Soviet space dog, Laika, who arrive on Earth decades later to find a way to save their alien planet Gersbach from being destroyed by a disturbance of gravity (D.O.G.).

Cameron, Eleanor. 1954. *The Wonderful Flight to the Mushroom Planet*. Boston: Little, Brown. Grades 4–6.
The classic featuring two boys who help a man from the planet Basidium build a space ship so he may return to help the Mushroom people. Sequels include *Stowaway to the Mushroom Planet* (1956), *Mr. Bass's Planetoid* (1958), and *A Mystery for Mr. Bass* (1960).

Dahl, Roald. 2001. *Charlie and the Great Glass Elevator.* Rev. ed. Illustrated by Quentin Blake. New York: Knopf. Grades 4–6.

The 1972 classic that takes Charlie Bucket, his family, and Willy Wonka to destinations unknown as they soar through the sky in a glass elevator.

Daley, Michael J. 2005. *Space Station Rat.* New York: Holiday House. Grades 4–6.

A laboratory rat, intelligent and trained to steal information and formulas, escapes, then stows away on a space station where he encounters the only child amidst the astronauts and scientists.

Johnson, David. 2007. *Trapped in Space.* Illustrated by Sonny Liew. Mankato, MN: Stone Arch Books. Grades 2–3.

When their space ship takes off without them, Sammi and Zak are stranded on a strange planet full of deadly spear plants.

Pratchett, Terry. 2005. *Only You Can Save Mankind: If Not You, Who Else?* New York: HarperCollins. Grades 5–8.

Against the backdrop of the Persian Gulf War, twelve-year-old Johnny plays a computer game that draws him closer to the reality of its alien female character ScreeWee.

Reeve, Philip. 2006. *Larklight, or, The Revenge of the White Spiders! or To rings and back!: A Rousing Tale of Dauntless Pluck in Farthest Reaches of Space.* New York: Bloomsbury. Grades 6–8.

Art and Myrtle Mumby live with their father on Larklight, a rambling house that flies through outer space. The arrival of White Spiders sets in motion a frenetic space-pirate adventure that includes pirate Jack Havock and an assortment of human-sized creatures.

Additional Summer Reading Theme Outlines

ReaDiscover Ancient Egypt: The World of the Pyramids and Pharaohs

A wealth of information is available on this intriguing topic that will have your summer readers exploring and recreating some of the major aspects of this time period. From their daily agricultural society to their religion, technology, writing, and art, ancient Egyptians led the way to discovering and creating ways to build, learn, and play.

Weeks 1 & 2—Live Like an Egyptian!

This unit can offer centers based on aspects of the Egyptians' hard-working and industrious society:

1. Housing—from mudbrick homes to a Pharaoh's palace
2. Clothing/Makeup/Jewelry—provide a taste of what was worn, and the importance of makeup and jewelry (collar or scarab motif necklace)
3. Food and Drink—how beer was made from barley, recipes including dried fruit and nuts
4. Farming—how the lunar calendar affected the three seasons of the year (Planting Time, Harvest Time, Flood Time)
5. Games and pastimes—examples of Senet and the Snake Board games, storytelling

Weeks 3 & 4—Pharaohs, Gods, and Mummies

1. Religion—Belief in numerous gods and goddesses, each with a different role, maintained peace and order in the land

   a. Explore some of the more important gods or goddesses

2. Life after death—how and why mummification was an important part of the religion
3. Burial chambers and the pyramids
4. Famous pharaohs and queens

   a. Sneferu/Hatshepsut/Ramses II/Cleopatra

Weeks 5 & 6—Learn Like an Egyptian!

1. Reading and writing and how Hieroglyphics have left clues to the past

   a. Hieroglyphs alphabet and activities

2. Math—Egyptians devised a measuring system using their bodies

   a. Creating a Cubit measuring stick
   b. Number writing system

3. Technology Egyptian style—How pyramids were designed and built using ramps and levers
4. Invention of a water clock

Weeks 7 & 8—Ancient Egyptian Arts and Crafts

Examples of the various trades and arts can be individual centers

1. Weaving and the making of a loom
2. Papermaking and papyrus scrolls
3. Pottery
4. Tomb painting

Initial Resources for Developing Interactive Centers for ReaDiscover Ancient Egypt: The World of the Pyramids and Pharaohs

Gibbons, Gail. 2004. *Mummies, Pyramids, and Pharaohs: A Book about Ancient Egypt.* New York: Little Brown.

Harris, Nathaniel. 2006. *Everyday Life in Ancient Egypt.* North Mankato, MN: Sea to Sea Publications.

Haslam, Andrew, and Alexandra Parsons. 1995. *Make It Work! Ancient Egypt.* New York: Thomson Learning.

Hodge, Susie. 1998. *Ancient Egyptian Art.* Des Plaines, IL: Heinemann Interactive Library.

Jorinelly, Joann, and Jason Netelkos. 2002. *The Crafts and Culture of the Ancient Egyptians.* New York: Rosen.

Landau, Elaine. 2005. *Exploring Ancient Egypt with Elaine Landau.* Berkeley Heights, NJ: Enslow.

Leech, Bonnie Coulter. 2007. *Pyramids.* New York: Rosen.

McCall, Henrietta. 2002. *Gods and Goddesses in the Daily Life of the Ancient Egyptians.* Illustrated by John James. Columbus, OH: Peter Bendrick Books.

Minnis, Ivan. 2005. *You Are in Ancient Egypt.* Chicago: Raintree.

Perl, Lila. 2004. *The Ancient Egyptians.* New York: Franklin Watts.

Solodky, M. 2006. *The Technology of Ancient Egypt.* New York: Rosen.

Winters, Kay. 2003. *Voices of Ancient Egypt.* Illustrated by Barry Moser. Washington, DC: National Geographic.

Wright, Rachel. 2005. *Egyptians: Facts, Things to Make, Activities.* North Mankato, MN: Sea to Sea Publications.

Web Sites

British Museum Ancient Egypt. http://www.ancientegypt.co.uk/menu.html.
Mark Millmore's Ancient Egypt. http://www.eyelid.co.uk/.

National Gallery of Art. The Quest for Immortality: The Treasures of Ancient Egypt. http://
   www.nga.gov/exhibitions/2002/egypt/.
University of Michigan School of Information. Mummies of Ancient Egypt. http://www.si.
   umich.edu/CHICO/mummy/.

A Seafaring Summer Adventure

Scientists often refer to the depths of the sea as "planet ocean," a part of earth that
is very difficult to explore and is still unknown or uncovered by man. This theme can
offer a fascinating look at what oceanographers do, how exploration continues, life
below the surface, the ocean's ecosystem, and mythology and lore, as well as historical
shipwrecks and discoveries.

Weeks 1 & 2—An Oceanographer's Quest

1. Ocean notions—Some incredible facts about the oceans and their geology
2. Diving to discover the inner space—tools and trade of the oceanographer
3. The various depths or levels below and their environments
4. Ocean or Sea? Differences or similarities

Weeks 3 & 4—Life Deep Below

1. Animals and sea creatures

   a. Blue whale—mammal or fish?

2. Plant life
3. Marine ecology
4. Ecosystems

Weeks 5 & 6—Sea Stories

1. Myths and legends
2. Daring adventures
3. Pirates and buccaneers

Weeks 7 & 8—Discovering Shipwrecks and Buried Treasure

1. The *Edmund Fitzgerald*
2. The *Titanic*
3. *Lusitania*
5. *Bismarck*
6. Scientists and explorers

*Initial Resources for Developing Interactive Centers for
a Seafaring Summer Adventure*

Burns, Loree Griffin. 2007. *Tracking Trash: Flotsam, Jetsam, and the Science of Ocean Motion.* Boston:
   Houghton Mifflin.
Gibbons, Gail. 1999. *Exploring the Deep, Dark Sea.* Boston: Little Brown.

Jedicke, Peter. 2003. *Exploring the Ocean Depths: The Final Frontier.* Mankato, MN: Smart Apple Media.

Johnson, Rebecca L. 2004. *A Journey into the Ocean.* Illustrations by Phyllis V. Saroff. Minneapolis: Carolrhoda Books.

Kozar, Richard. 1999. *Infamous Pirates.* Philadelphia: Chelsea House.

Littlefield, Cindy A. 2003. *Awesome Ocean Science! Investigating the Secrets of the Underwater World.* Illustrations by Sarah Rakatin. Charlotte, VT: Williamson Pub.

Matsen, Bradford. 2003. *The Incredible Quest to Find the Titanic.* Berkley Heights, NJ: Enslow.

———. 2003. *The Incredible Quest to Find the Atocha.* Berkley Heights, NJ: Enslow.

Mauffret, Yvon. 2003. *The Sea: Exploring Life on an Ocean Planet.* Adapted by Robert Burleigh. Photographs by Philip Plisson. Drawings by Emmanuel Cerisier. New York: Harry Abrams.

Nye, Bill. 1999. *Bill Nye the Science Guy's Big Blue Ocean.* Additional writing by Ian G. Saunders. Illustrated by John S. Dykes. New York: Hyperion Books for Children.

Polking, Kirk. 1999. *Oceanographers and Explorers of the Sea.* Springfield, NJ: .Enslow.

Ross, Stewart. 1995. *Pirates: The Story of Buccaneers, Brigands, Corsairs, and Their Piracy on the High Seas from the Spanish Main to the China Sea.* Brookfield, CT: Copper Beech Books.

Scholastic Reference. 2004. *Scholastic Atlas of Oceans.* New York: Scholastic Reference.

Vieira, Linda. 2003. *The Seven Seas: Exploring the World Ocean.* Illustrated by Higgins Bond. New York: Walker.

Wargin, Kathy-Jo. 2003. *The Edmund Fitzgerald: Song of the Bell.* Illustrated by Gijsbert van Frankenhoyzen. Chelsea, MI: Sleeping Bear Press.

DVD/Video Recording

Ocean. Written and produced by Bill Butt. Eyewitness DVD Series. New York: DK Publishing, 2006.

Web Sites

Discovery School Planet Ocean. http://school.discoveryeducation.com/schooladventures/planetocean/index.html.

Smithsonian Institution. Traveling Exhibit: Ocean Planet. http://www.smithsonianeducation.org/educators/lesson_plans/ocean/main.html.

Let's Make Music! A Summer in Symphony and Song

From ancient instruments to classical, from modern day jazz, rock, rhythm and blues to hip hop, music is a part of life. Everyone identifies with music in some way, through song, instruments, radio, or favorite music artists. Your musical summer can include musical styles, cultural influences, the science and sound of music, and musical math and notation, as well as popular artists and, of course, stories in song.

Weeks 1 & 2—What Makes Music?

1. How did music develop?
2. Ancient instruments
3. Early musicians
4. Sounds, science, and math of music
5. Music technology old and new

Weeks 3 & 4—Around the World in Music

Instruments unique to each culture

1. African
2. Asian
3. Native American
4. Aborigine
5. Middle Eastern

Weeks 5 & 6—Musical Genres

Musical notation and instruments unique to each

1. Classical
2. Jazz/R&B
3. Rock
4. Folk
5. Famous musicians within each genre

Weeks 7 & 8—Musical Story

1. Opera/Operetta—characters and story for an opera such as *The Magic Flute*
2. Dance—story told in ballet or even modern dance, such as *The Lion King*
3. Musicals—How a cartoon like Peanuts is turned into theater—"You're a Good Man Charlie Brown"
4. Classical/Orchestral such as Serge Prokofieff's "Peter and the Wolf"

Initial Resources for Developing Interactive Centers for Let's Make Music! A Summer in Symphony and Song

Adler, Naomi. 1997. *Play Me A Story: Nine Tales About Musical Instruments.* Brookfield, CT: Millbrook Press.

Ardley, Neil. 2004. *Music.* New York: DK Publishing.

Barber, Nicola. 2001. *Music: An A–Z Guide.* New York: Franklin Watts.

Dunleavy Deborah. 2001. *The Kids Can Press Jumbo Book of Music.* Illustrated by Louise Phillips. Toronto: Kids Can Press.

Hart, Avery. 1993. *Kids Make Music! Clapping and Tapping from Bach to Rock!* Illustrated by Loretta Trezzo Braren. Charlotte, VT: Williamson.

Kallen, Stuart. 2003. *The Instruments of Music.* San Diego: Lucent Books.

Levine, Robert. 2001. *The Story of the Orchestra: Listen While You Learn about the Instruments, the Music, and the Composers Who Wrote the Music.* Illustrated by Meredith Hamilton. New York: Black Dog & Leventhal.

O'Brien, Eileen. 2006. *Usborne Introduction to Music.* New York: Scholastic.

Sabbeth, Alex. 1997. *Rubber-Band Banjos and a Java Jive Bass: Projects and Activities on the Science of Music and Sound.* Illustrations by Laurel Aiello. New York: Wiley.

Web Sites

Energy in the Air: Sounds from the Orchestra. http://library.thinkquest.org/5116/.

Jazz/PBS Kids Go. http://pbskids.org/jazz/index.html.

Music Notes: An Interactive Online Musical Experience. http://library.thinkquest.org/15413/.
Music in Numbers. http://reglos.de/musinum/.
National Music Museum. http://www.usd.edu/smm/galleries.html.

Summer Safari: Animals and Folklore of the African Kingdom

Take your summer readers on an African safari tour with this theme, which includes African cultures, animals, plants, and folklore. You can explore the specifics of an observational safari tour, the many animals and their natural habitats, endangered species, and the folklore of Africa that has inspired many of the stories outside the continent, as far as South America, the Caribbean, and the United States.

Weeks 1 & 2—Safari Basics

1. Safari know-how
2. Equipment to take along: binoculars, cameras, special clothing, etc.
3. Photography tips
4. Safari Diary

Weeks 3 & 4—On the Safari Trail

Game viewing

1. Endangered animals
2. Specific species
3. Animal migration
4. Plants of the desert environment

Weeks 5 & 6—African Folklore

1. Tricksters
2. Morals
3. Pourquoi

Weeks 7 & 8—Stories in the African Diaspora

1. African American

   a. Trickster, Conjure, Flight, Moral Supernatural, Pourquoi

2. Caribbean

   a. Animal tricksters (Anansi)

3. South American

   a. Supernatural and Pourquoi

Initial Resources for Developing Interactive Centers for
Summer Safari: Animals and Folklore of the African Kingdom

Badoe, Adwoa. 2001. *The Pot of Wisdom: Ananse Stories.* Illustrated by Baba Wagué Diakité. Toronto: Groundwood.
Bateman, Robert, and Rick Archbold. 1998. *Safari.* Boston: Little Brown.

Croze, Harvey. 2006. *Africa for Kids: Exploring a Vibrant Continent 19 Activities.* Chicago: Chicago Review Press.

Hamilton, Virginia. 1997. *A Ring of Tricksters: Animal Tales from America, the West Indies, and Africa.* Illustrated by Barry Moser. New York: Blue Sky Press.

Hatkoff, Isabella, Hatkoff, Craig, and Kahumbu, Paula. 2007. *Owen & Mzee: The Language of Friendship.* New York: Scholastic.

Lindblad, Lisa. 1994. *The Serengeti Migration: African Animals on the Move.* New York: Hyperion.

McGill, Alice. 2004. *Sure as Sunrise: Stories of Bruh Rabbit and His Walkin' Talkin' Friends.* Illustrated by Don Tate. Boston: Houghton Mifflin.

National Geographic Society. 2003. *African Adventure Atlas.* Evergreen, Colorado: National Geographic Society.

Thompson, Gare. 2006. *Serengeti Journey: On Safari in Africa.* Washington, DC: National Geographic Society.

Turner, Pamela. 2005. *Gorilla Doctors: Saving Endangered Great Apes.* Boston: Houghton Mifflin.

Washington, Donna L. 2004. *A Pride of African Tales.* Illustrated by James Ransome. New York: HarperCollins.

Web Sites

Africa Geographia. http://www.geographia.com/indx06.htm.

African Wildlife Foundation. http://www.awf.org/section/wildlife/gallery.

National Geographic Society. http://animals.nationalgeographic.com/.

PBS Kids Africa for Kids. http://pbskids.org/africa/index.html.

Westward Ho! Catch the Pioneer Spirit

America's exciting expansion to territories west of St. Louis is a theme that can delve into the lifestyle on the westward trail, pioneer homesteading, storytelling, and Gold Rush fever.

Weeks 1 & 2—Life on the Trail

1. Lewis & Clark—first explorations and discovery
2. Transportation—Conestoga wagons to stagecoach travel
3. Campfires—food and song
4. Travel routes—Oregon, Santa Fe, Chisholm trails
5. Animals on the trail

Weeks 3 & 4—Pioneer and Western Living

1. Housing—creating a log home
2. Schools—learning
3. Foods—from crops to kettle
4. Cowboys, trappers, and traders
5. Getting the mail—The Pony Express
6. Outlaws and lawmen—Taming the Wild West

Weeks 5 & 6—Folklore of the West

1. American tall tales
2. Campfire stories
3. Native American myths

Weeks 7 & 8—Gold Rush!

1. James Marshall and John Sutter's mill—how it all started
2. Gold diggers and prospectors—panning and other ways to find gold

    a. Tools and treasures

3. Life in a mining town
4. Klondike gold—Alaska and its riches

Initial Resources for Developing Interactive Centers for Westward Ho! Catch the Pioneer Spirit

Carlson, Laurie. 1996. *Westward Ho! An Activity Guide to the Wild West.* Chicago: Chicago Review Press.

Daniel, Charlie. 1997. *By the Light of the Moon: Campfire Songs and Cowboy Tunes.* CD. New York: Sony Wonder.

Erdosh, George. 1997. *Food and Recipes of the Westward Expansion.* New York: Rosen.

Galford, Ellen. 2005. *The Trail West: Exploring History through Art.* Chanhassen, MN: Two-Can Publishing, 2005.

Hill, Maureen. 1998. *Wild West: The History and Myths of the American West Explained in Glorious Colour.* London: Caxton Editions.

Isserman, Maurice and John S. Bowman, eds. 2005. *Across America: The Lewis and Clark Expedition.* New York: Facts on File.

Johmann, Carol A., and Elizabeth J. Rieth. 2000. *Going West! Journey on a Wagon Train to Settle a Frontier Town.* Illustrated by Michael Kline. Charlotte, VT: Williamson Publishing.

Josephson, Judith Pinkerton. 2003. *Growing Up in Pioneer America 1800–1890.* Minneapolis: Lerner.

King, David C. 1997. *Pioneer Days: Discover the Past with Fun Projects, Games, Activities, and Recipes.* New York: John Wiley.

Miller, Brandon Marie. 1995. *Buffalo Gals: Women of the Old West.* Minneapolis: Lerner.

Morley, Jacqueline. 1995. *How Would You Survive in the American West?* Illustrated by David Antram. New York: Franklin Watts.

Murray, Stuart. 2001. *Wild West.* London: DK Publishing.

Schanzer, Rosalyn. 1999. *Gold Fever: Tales from the California Gold Rush.* Washington, DC: National Geographic Society.

Web Sites

American West. http://www.americanwest.com/.

New Perspectives on the West. http://www.pbs.org/weta/thewest/.

Oakland Museum of California. Gold Rush! http://www.museumca.org/goldrush/.

U.S. Westward Expansion. http://www.besthistorysites.net/USHistory_WestwardExpansion.html.

List of Reproducible Graphics

Index

About the Author

RITA SOLTAN, an experienced children's librarian, worked in public libraries in New York and Michigan for more than 30 years. She holds a BA in Education/Spanish Literature, an MLS from Queens College of the City University of New York, and a Master of Arts in Teaching Reading and Language Arts from Oakland University in Rochester, Michigan. She conducts numerous workshops for librarians, teachers, and parents using literature throughout the curriculum and is currently an adjunct instructor at Oakland Community College in Southeast Michigan. Rita has published several articles on children's services and literature, reviews for *Kirkus Reviews, Horn Book Guide,* and *School Library Journal,* and is the author of *Reading Raps: A Book Club Guide for Librarians, Kids, and Families* (Libraries Unlimited, 2005).

About the Illustrator

JILL REICHENBACH FILL holds a BS from Michigan State University. She has been a freelance graphic artist for over 20 years and has won numerous national awards for her designs.